Fish and Other Aquatic Resource Trends in the United States

A Technical Document Supporting the Forest Service 2010 RPA Assessment

Andrew J. Loftus and Curtis H. Flather

I0434822

Abstract: The Forest and Rangeland Renewable Resources Planning Act (RPA) of 1974 requires periodic assessments of the status and trends in the Nation's renewable natural resources including fish and other aquatic species and their habitats. Data from a number of sources are used to document trends in habitat quality, populations, resource use, and patterns of imperilment among aquatic fauna. Freshwater habitat quality varied widely across the United States. Nationwide, more than half of monitored lakes were ranked in good condition, but the percentage ranged from a high of 91 percent in the upper Midwest to a low of 1 percent in the Northern Plains. Habitat conditions in monitored small streams indicated that 42 percent were found to be in poor condition. The Southern Appalachians, Southern Plains, and Northern Plains have 50 percent or more of their stream lengths in poor condition. The condition of small stream habitats was best in the Western mountains. Data availability continues to limit comprehensive evaluations of freshwater fish populations. Of the 253 marine fish stocks assessed in 2009, 38 percent were deemed to be overfished or subject to overfishing. Pacific salmon have declined throughout much of their range although stocks native to Alaska have fared better than those in the Pacific Northwest. Species associated with aquatic habitats have higher proportions of species considered to be at-risk of extinction than other species groups. At-risk aquatic species are concentrated in watersheds occurring in the southern Appalachians and the southeastern coastal plain. The number of anglers has declined since the early 1990s. Relationships between land use, water quality, and aquatic species conditions are explored in a series of case studies. The report provides implications of aquatic resource trends for management and planning.

Authors

Andrew J. Loftus is a natural resource consultant at 3116 Munz Drive, Suite A, Annapolis, MD; **Curtis H. Flather** is a research ecologist at the Rocky Mountain Research Station in Fort Collins, CO.

Acknowledgments

This work was supported by the Forest Service Research and Development's RPA research program as part of the Forest Service's national assessment reporting requirements mandated by the Forest and Rangeland Renewable Resources Planning Act. The document benefited from constructive reviews received from Dr. Craig Paukert (USGS Missouri Cooperative Fish and Wildlife Research Unit, University of Missouri), Dr. Nancy Leonard (Northwest Power and Conservation Council), and Dr. Linda Langner (USDA Forest Service). We also wish to thank Michael S. Knowles (U.S. Forest Service, Rocky Mountain Research Station) for data analysis and graphics support, Lane Eskew for editing the final document, Richard Aiken (U.S. Fish and Wildlife Service) for unpublished data on angler participation status and trends, Dr. Nancy Nate (University of Wisconsin-Stevens Point) and Andrea Ostroff (U.S. Geological Survey) for contributions to the case studies, Dr. Tom Sminkey and Dr. Alan Lowther (National Marine Fisheries Service) for assistance with marine fisheries statistics, Jeff Smith (Morrisinformatics LLC) for graphics support, and Jason McNees (NatureServe) for his assistance with at-risk species associated with aquatic habitats.

Contents

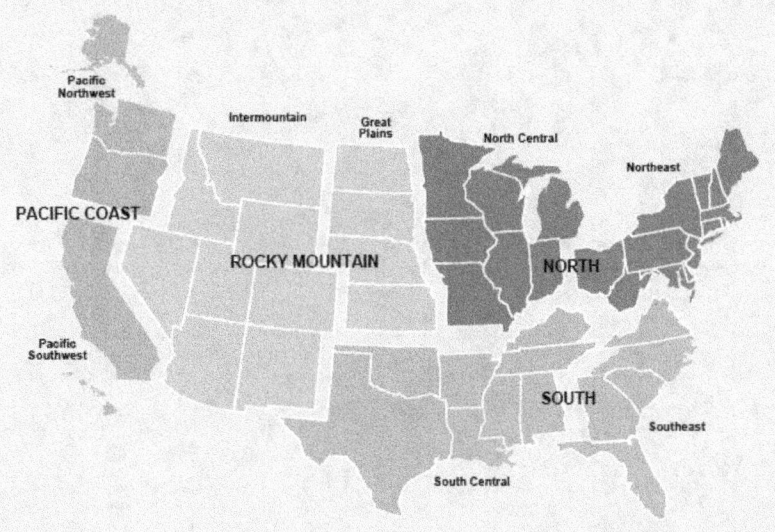

Introduction

Aquatic ecosystems provide a variety of ecological services and economic benefits to society (see Appendix A for a glossary of terms). These range from products as fundamental as safe drinking water to healthy and abundant fish populations that provide food for consumers and sustain leisure opportunities for recreational anglers.

The ecological condition of these resources is driven by many factors. Aquatic systems are the recipients of the byproducts from activities in the surrounding landscape and are also affected by inputs that can originate from well outside the local ecosystem. Nonpoint pollution delivery is affected by land cover, forest and rangeland management, and agricultural activities within watersheds (Allan and others 1997) and freshwater ecosystems are particularly affected by the introduction of exotic species originating from intercontinental exchanges (Rahel 2002). Furthermore, aquatic systems are often collection points for elements from atmospheric deposition. As such, the biotic communities in these systems are heavily influenced by forces external to their immediate surroundings (Kennen and others 2005). At the same time, aquatic systems can also serve as delivery mechanisms, transporting the accumulation of atmospheric deposition, nutrients, and runoff from the surrounding watershed thousands of miles away to feed other aquatic systems as well as depositing the sediments that they carry on flooded landscapes far away from their original source. Thus, input from the farthest inland reaches of the continental United States can influence the health of aquatic biota in the estuarine and marine ecosystems of America's coastland.

These external influences that may originate in distant landscapes present challenges to managers of aquatic systems around the United States (Fausch and others 2002). The dynamic linkage between landscapes and aquatic conditions is nothing new, but the speed at which changes can occur before management can react has generally increased with the evolution of industrial society. For this reason, periodic evaluations of the current aquatic resource condition (status) and an analysis of how resource conditions have changed over time (trends) are a necessary prerequisite for science-based management and policy decisions. This report provides an overview of the information that is available on the status and trends of fisheries and aquatic resources, identifies information gaps that impede the assessment of status and trends, and highlights some of the large scale landscape processes that are threatening aquatic ecosystems today.

This report is motivated by the Forest and Rangeland Renewable Resources Planning Act of 1974 (RPA) as amended by the National Forest Management Act of 1976. The RPA directs the Forest Service to prepare periodic national assessments of the current and expected renewable natural resource situation on all of the nation's forest and range lands. Fish and other living aquatic resources, and the habitats on which they depend, are an important aspect of these resource assessments, particularly as managers move to a more holistic ecosystem approach and strive to sustain the goods and services that the public derives from aquatic systems.

We review trends in several attributes of aquatic resources including aquatic habitat, fish populations, harvests, and participants in recreational and commercial fisheries. We report national summaries of emerging trends and, to the extent that the data permit, regional aquatic resource trends for each of the four RPA Assessment Regions (Figure 1). In some

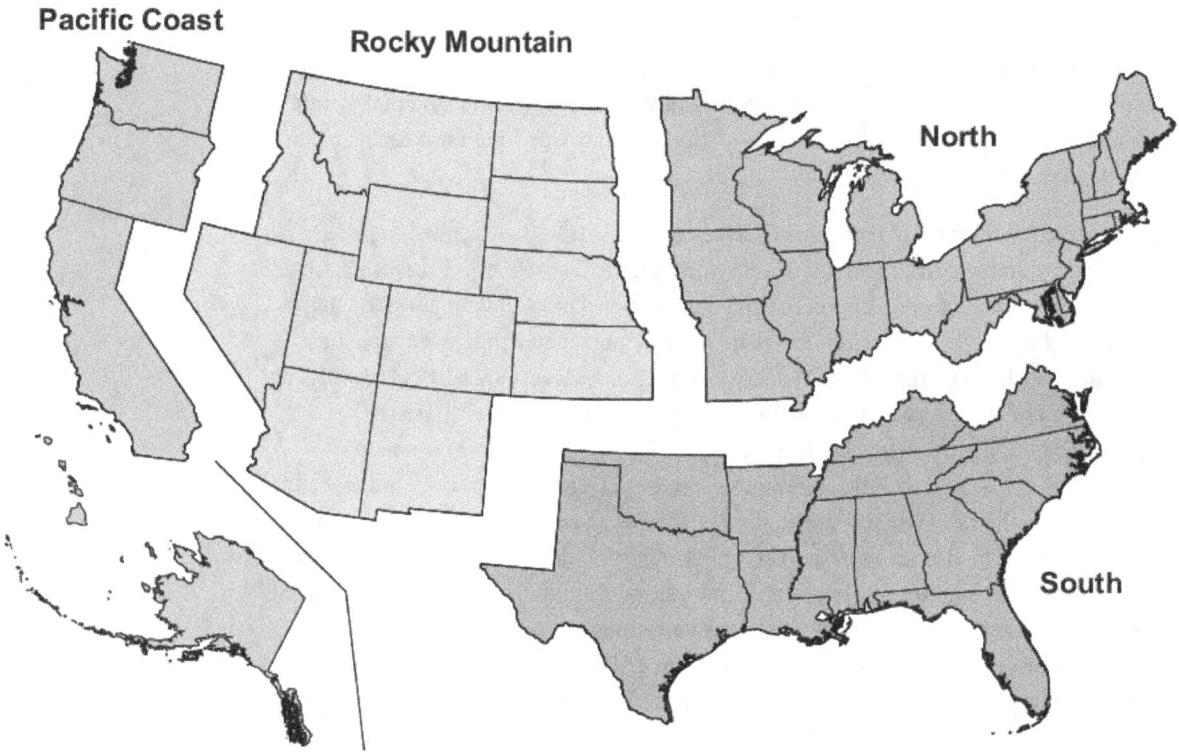

Figure 1—Forest Service RPA Assessment regions.

instances, data on aquatic resources have been reported for regions that could not be aggregated to conform to the RPA regions defined in Figure 1. For this reason, we also present aquatic resource trends for other geographic regions when they are well-established in aquatic resource monitoring (for example, EPA ecoregions).

The RPA directs that an assessment of resources and utilization occurring on all lands of all ownership be conducted, not just on lands for which the USDA Forest Service has primary resource stewardship responsibility. Therefore, case studies and population assessments are provided here for a variety of lands, including near-shore marine species. Previous RPA assessments have noted that aquatic systems face serious threats from changing landscape practices (Loftus and Flather 2000). While this is still true in 2010, scientists and managers have more information available today for assessing these threats and formulating possible actions to directly address or mitigate them. However, this report is not a detailed accounting of the status of every aquatic resource in the United States and as such differs from some other resource assessment documents prepared for the RPA. As we discuss later, the information needed to make such analyses and determinations is incomplete and difficult to access. This report does focus on the general condition of aquatic habitats, species (see Appendix B for scientific names of species mentioned in this report), and usage trends as reflected by the results of existing surveys and data collection efforts. Supplementing this are case studies that predominately focus on landscape or environmental agents impacting aquatic species status and trends. Intertwined throughout the document, and highlighted in special sections, are the socioeconomic benefits attributable to maintaining healthy aquatic ecosystems.

Trends in Fish Habitat and Populations _____

Freshwater Resources in the United States

There are over 3.5 million miles of freshwater rivers and streams and 39.9 million acres of lakes and reservoirs (excluding Great Lakes) in the United States (USEPA 2006, 2009a). These aquatic systems play a vital role in the economic, social, and ecological framework of the country. Freshwater lakes and reservoirs provide 70 percent of the drinking water of the United States, hydropower for industry, irrigation for agriculture, and transportation corridors for shipping among other anthropogenic uses.[1] Ecologically, freshwater resources provide vital habitat that supports freshwater and estuarine fish populations, aquatic species of conservation concern, and other aquatic flora and fauna that constitute healthy aquatic ecosystems which in turn support commercial and recreational fishing activities.

Lake and Stream Conditions

In 2004-2005, the U.S. EPA conducted an assessment of chemical, physical, and biological attributes of 1,392 "wadeable," perennial stream locations in the United States to determine the biological condition of those waters (USEPA 2006). These streams constitute approximately 90 percent of the stream and river miles in the coterminous United States. In 2007, the EPA completed the National Lakes Assessment (NLA) evaluating the condition of natural and human-made freshwater lakes, ponds, and reservoirs greater than 10 acres in size in the coterminous United States, excluding the Great Lakes (USEPA 2009). A total of 1,028 lakes were sampled during summer 2007, representing the condition of about 50,000 lakes nationwide (excluding the Great Lakes and Great Salt Lake). Taken together, these two assessments constitute the most comprehensive scientifically based evaluation of the freshwater resources of these 48 states.

The biological condition of lake and stream habitats was measured by the percentage of taxa observed compared to those that are expected based on reference conditions in least-disturbed aquatic systems (USEPA 2006, 2009a) – also called the Observed/Expected (O/E) ratio of taxa loss. Measurements of stream conditions were supplemented with a second measure, the Macroinvertebrate Index of Biotic Condition (MIBC). The MIBC is based on the Index of Biotic Integrity developed for fish in Midwestern streams that was modified for other regions, taxonomic groups, and ecosystems. The MIBC incorporates measures of taxonomic richness, composition, and diversity as well as feeding groups, pollution tolerance, and life history traits.

Lake ratings were based on an O/E index of phytoplankton and zooplankton taxa loss. The wadeable streams survey rated condition based on O/E ratios and MIBC of benthic macroinvertebrates. The results of these assessments are broken down into three regions and nine ecoregions (Figure 2) with the rating scales summarized in Table 1. Overall, 22 percent of the lakes and 42 percent of wadeable streams were rated in "poor condition" while 56 percent and 28 percent respectively were rated as being in "good" condition (Table 2).

---

[1] US Environmental Protection Agency http://water.epa.gov/type/lakes/, October 24, 2011.

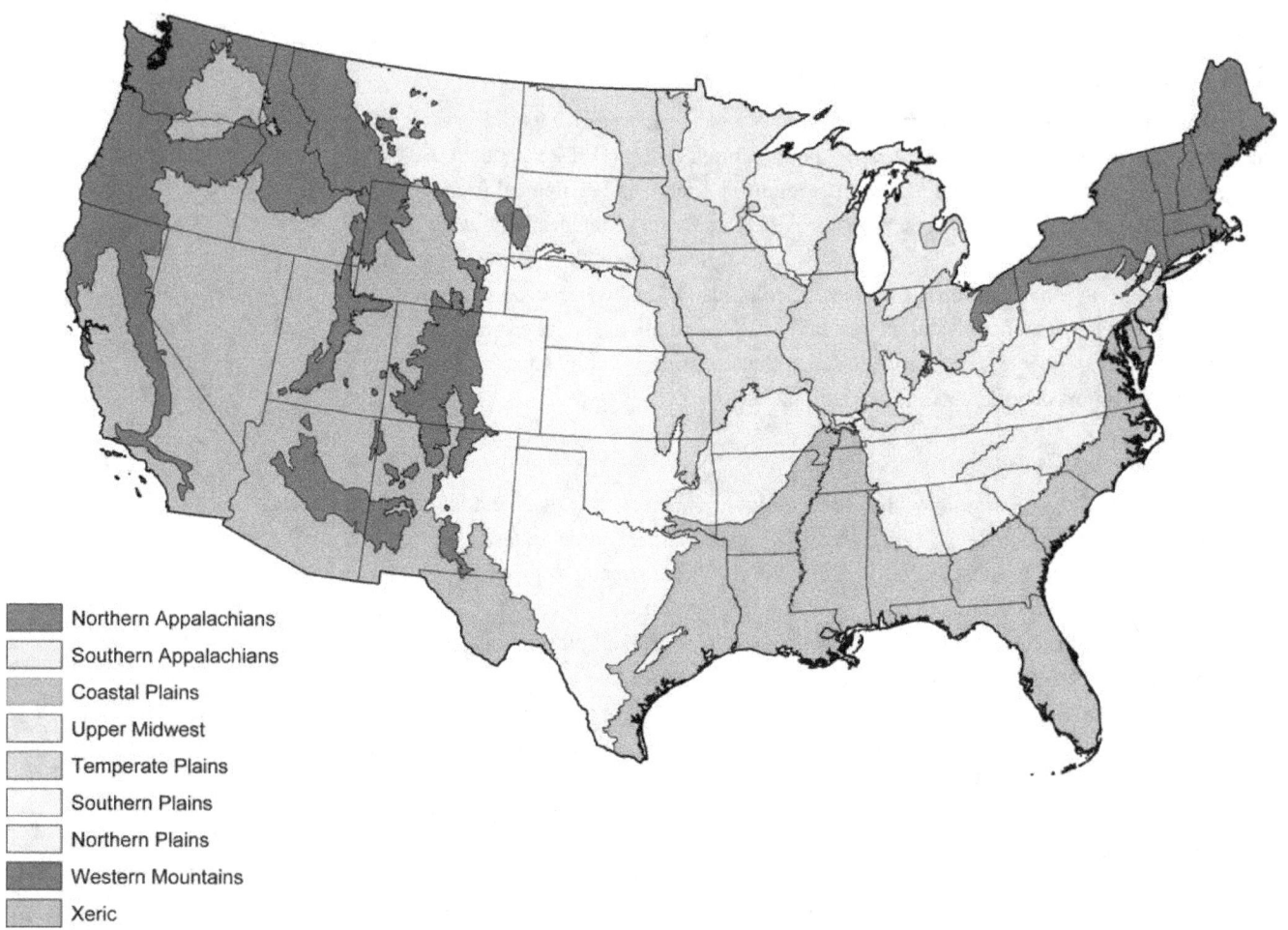

Northern Appalachians
Southern Appalachians
Coastal Plains
Upper Midwest
Temperate Plains
Southern Plains
Northern Plains
Western Mountains
Xeric

Figure 2—Ecoregions surveyed by the EPA Wadeable Streams Assessment.

Table 1—Condition ratings used to assess habitat quality of lakes and streams across the coterminous United States. Stream habitat condition is measured by macroinvertebrate taxa loss determined by the ratio of observed number of species (O) to the number of species expected at least-disturbed reference sites (E).

| Rating | Waterbody type | |
	Lakes (> 10 ac)	Streams (wadeable)
Good	<20 percent taxa loss (O/E>0.80)	Stream condition as good as or better than 75% of reference sites
Fair	20-40 percent taxa loss	Stream condition worse than 75% but better than 5% of reference condition
Poor	>40 percent taxa loss (O/E<0.60)	Stream condition worse than 95% of reference sites

Table 2—Status of the biological condition of lakes and impoundments greater than 10 acres and small streams in the United States (USEPA 2006, 2009). Numbers in parenthesis indicate number of lakes or miles of streams in the United States.

Ranking	Natural lakes (29,308)	Human-made lakes (20,238)	All lakes (49,546)	Wadeable streams (671,051 miles)
Good condition	66.5%	40.4%	55.8%	28.2%
Fair condition	16.3%	28.8%	21.4%	24.9%
Poor condition	16.8%	30.4%	22.3%	41.9%

The Upper Midwest had by far the greatest number of lakes rated as "good" biological condition (91 percent). The Northern Plains region, where Federal lands account for nearly 26 percent of the total area, had the greatest number of lakes rated as "poor" biological condition with 90 percent of the lakes in that category (Table 3). Lake shorelines in this region exhibit very high levels of disturbance due to human activities, with 90 percent of lakes having moderate or high lakeshore human disturbance. This anthropogenic disturbance fosters increased sedimentation and runoff and elevated nutrient inputs. Total phosphorus and nitrogen concentrations were poor in 71 percent and 91 percent of lakes respectively in the Northern Plains region. Additionally, microcystin (a toxin to humans, plants, and wildlife) was present in one third of lakes and at levels of concern in 1 percent of lakes. Analysis of fish tissue contaminants (collected as part of another study) showed mercury concentrations in game fish exceeded health-based limits in 49 percent of lakes, and polychlorinated biphenyls (PCBs) were found at potential levels of concern in 17 percent of lakes (fish consumption advisories are discussed in more detail later in this report). A comparison of these results to comparable studies in the 1970s revealed that 75 percent of the 800 lakes sampled in the 1970s showed either improvements or no change in phosphorus levels in the 2007 study (USEPA 2009). There is some evidence that reservoirs may facilitate the spread of exotic aquatic organisms throughout a landscape (Havel and others 2005).

Table 3—Status of the biological condition of lakes > 10 acres by region in the United States based on planktonic O/E taxa loss (USEPA 2006).

Region	Number of lakes in each region	Condition (% of lakes)		
		Good	Fair	Poor
Nationwide	49,546	56	21	22
Northern Appalachians	5,226	55	30	15
Southern Appalachians	4,690	42	27	31
Coastal Plains	7,009	47	25	27
Upper Midwest	15,562	91	5	4
Temperate Plains	6,327	24	40	35
Southern Plains	3,148	34	36	29
Northern Plains	2,660	1	6	90
Western Mountains	4,122	58	31	11
Xeric West/Southwest	802	35	14	49

On a regional basis, the Western streams were in the best biological condition (45 percent of stream length in good condition), the Plains and Lowlands region next with 30 percent of stream length in good condition, and the Eastern Highlands in the poorest condition with only 18 percent of stream length in good condition (Table 4).

Table 4—Status of small streams (percent of stream miles in each condition), by region in the coterminous United States (USEPA 2006).

Condition	Western Region (152,425 miles)	Plains and Lowlands (242,264 miles)	Eastern Highlands (376,362 miles)
Good	45.1	29.0	18.2
Fair	25.8	29.0	20.5
Poor	27.4	40	51.8

On an ecoregional basis, the Southern Plains, Southern Appalachians, and Northern Plains regions exhibited the greatest percentage of streams rated in "poor" condition with over 50 percent of the streams in those regions in this category based on the Macroinvertebrate Index of Biotic Condition (Figure 3). In terms of macroinvertebrate taxa loss based on the O/E ratio, the Appalachian complex (Northern and Southern Appalachian ecoregions) had the highest percentage of stream miles exhibiting greater than 50 percent loss (Figure 4). As with lakes, the factors having the greatest impact on streams in all of the regions were elevated nutrients (nitrogen and phosphorus), riparian disturbance (defined as non-existent or a simplified network of vegetative cover along the stream bank), and streambed sediments. The risk of assigning a stream a condition ranking of "poor" was two times greater for streams that were subject to these threats than for streams that were assigned a rank of "good" (USEPA 2006).

Great Lakes

The Great Lakes constitute the largest system of surface freshwater on earth. The five Great Lakes and connecting waters contain approximately 20 percent of the earth's freshwater and 90 percent of the surface freshwater in the United States. Considering the large geographic coverage of the lakes, and their multiple political jurisdictions spanning two national boundaries and eight state boundaries, there is no single assessment of water quality or habitat condition that can characterize the state of the lakes. However, extensive collaboration between jurisdictions has resulted in a compilation of assessments that can be applied to this purpose. Human settlement within the watersheds of the lakes ranges from relatively sparse areas of the northern regions of Lake Superior to some of the most densely populated urban centers including Chicago, Detroit, Buffalo, Cleveland, and other areas of the southern parts of the region. With this range of settlement patterns, each region in the Great Lakes basin faces unique sets of challenges to water quality and habitat condition. To varying degrees, all areas face major stresses of toxic and nutrient pollution, invasive species, and habitat degradation. Pollution sources include sedimentation and agricultural pollutants, industrial discharges, runoff and waste water discharges from urban areas, and pollutants from atmospheric deposition.

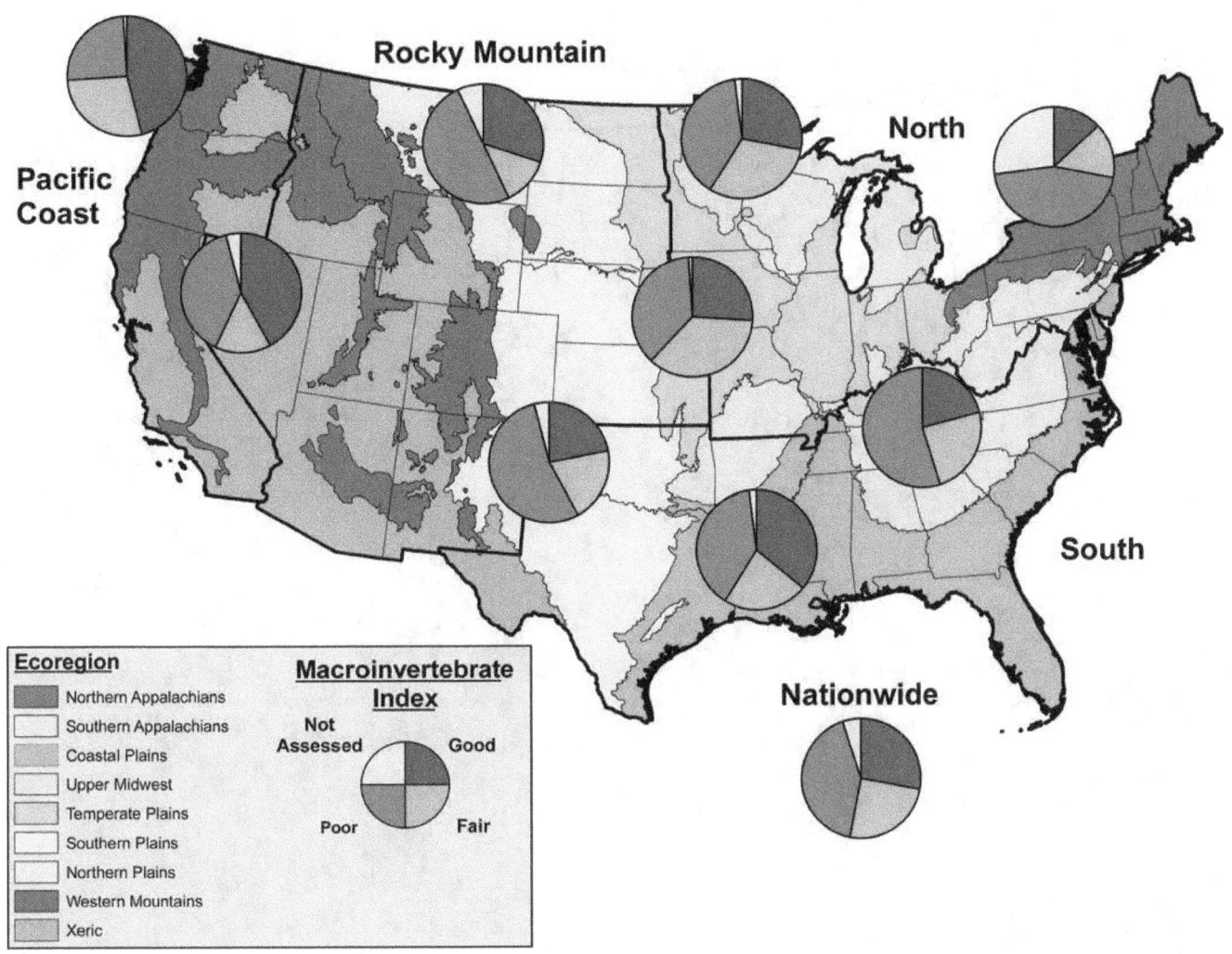

Figure 3—Stream biological condition as measured by the Macroinvertebrate Index of Biotic Condition in the EPA Wadeable Stream Survey. See Appendix C for source data values.

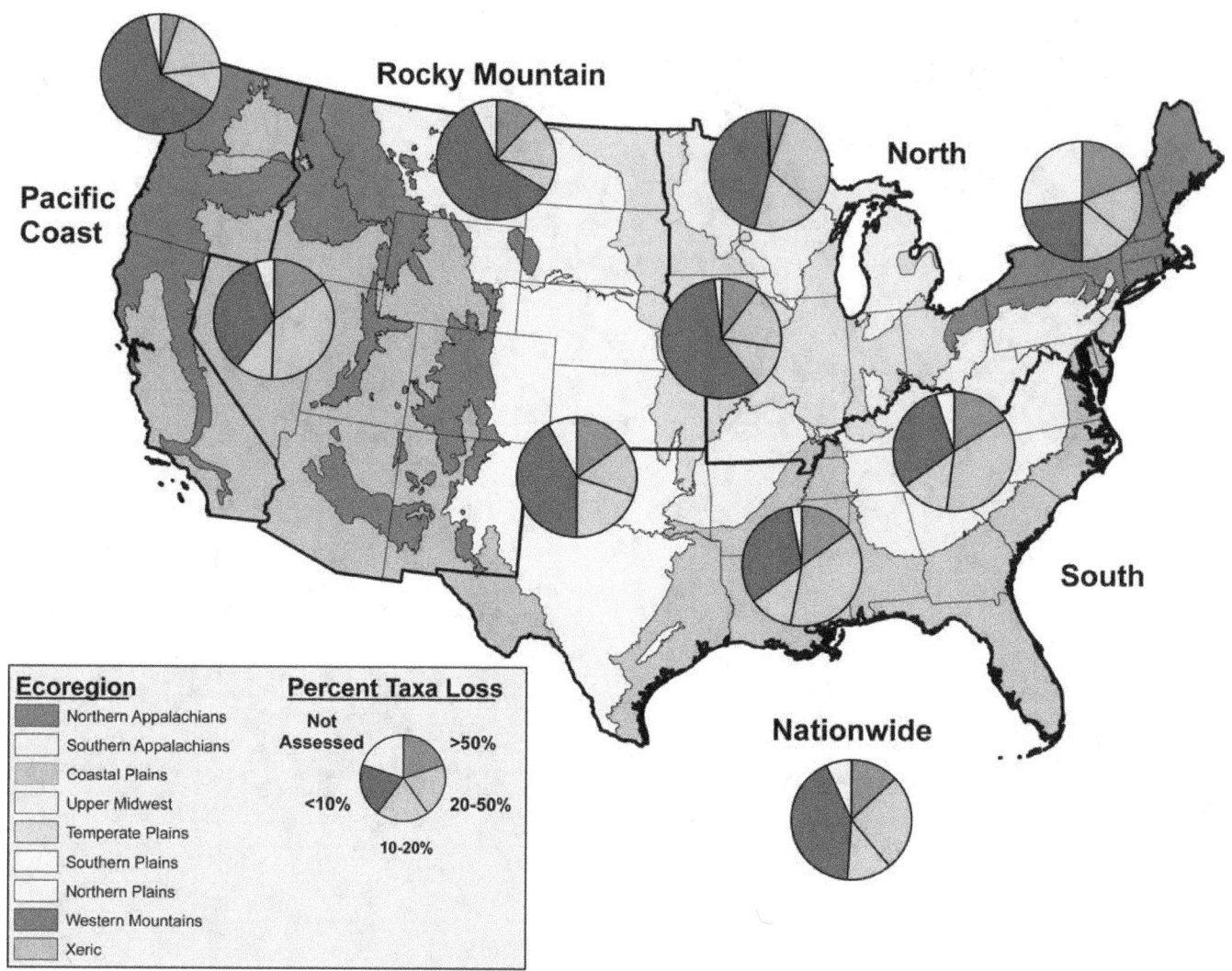

Figure 4—Stream habitat condition as measured by macroinvertebrate taxa loss determined by the ratio of observed number of species (O) to the number of species expected at least-disturbed reference sites (E) within each ecoregion. Pie charts indicate the proportion of stream lengths in various classes of taxa loss. The " >50%" class indicates that more than half the expected species from least-disturbed reference sites were lost (undetected in surveys), and the " <10%" class indicates that fewer than 10% of the expected species were lost from surveyed streams. See Appendix D for source data values.

Overall, Great Lakes coastal condition is rated as fair to poor in all five of the lakes and connecting waterways (Table 5). In 2008, a compilation of environmental indicator reports was assembled for the "State of the Lakes Ecosystem Conference" in Niagara Falls, Ontario. These indices produced mixed results for status and trends for the nine indicators measured, due largely to the diversity of habitats and stressors across the Great Lakes basin (Table 6) (USEPA and Environment Canada 2009). Additionally the effects of climate change were identified as a concern and emerging influence although no assessment was presented for the "status" or "trends" of that factor.

Further breaking these results down to a lake-by-lake basis reveals both the previously mentioned commonalities of stressors and the particular factors affecting each lake (Table 7).

Table 5—Great Lakes coastal condition based on five indices (USEPA 2008).

Index	Rating
Water quality (eutrophic condition, water clarity, dissolved oxygen levels, phosphorus concentrations)	Fair
Fish tissue contaminants (concentrations of PCBs, mercury, chlordane, dioxin, and toxaphene)	Fair
Sediment quality (toxic contamination)	Poor
Coastal habitat (amphibian and wetland-dependent bird abundance and diversity, extent of coastal wetlands)	Poor
Benthic community	Poor

Table 6—Status and trends of environmental indicators for the Great Lakes basin (USEPA and Environment Canada 2009).

Indicator	Status	Trends
Coastal Zones and Aquatic Habitats	Mixed	Undetermined
Invasive Species	Poor	Deteriorating
Contamination (toxic chemicals)	Mixed	Improving
Human Health (drinking water, consumption advisories)	Mixed	Undetermined
Status of Biotic Communities	Mixed	Undetermined
Resource Utilization (water withdrawals, energy consumption, urbanization)	Mixed	Undetermined
Land Use-Land Cover	Mixed	Undetermined

Table 7—General condition and highlighted stressors of each of the Great Lakes (USEPA and Environment Canada 2009)

Lake	Condition	Stresses
Superior	Ecosystem is in generally good condition	Non-native species, toxic chemicals and fish consumption advisories, shoreline development and hardening, habitat loss, land use change, mining, and climate change effects.
Michigan	Notable return of bird, mammal and aquatic species due to habitat restoration and dam removal and a continued decline of contaminants in fish.	Major food web disruption, viral hemorrhagic septicemia in fish, invasive quagga mussel, detrimental algae growth, water levels below average.
Erie	Yellow perch stocks are recovering; walleye, lake trout, and lake whitefish are struggling. PCBs and mercury continue to affect fish consumption. Zebra mussels, quagga mussels, round gobies, and predatory zooplankton, are changing the food web.	Nutrient management remains the top priority for improving the lake.
Ontario	The reduction in contaminants continues to improve.	Zebra mussels, quagga mussels, and predatory zooplankton have become established and are impacting food web dynamics. Nearshore algal blooms, resulting in beach closures, drinking water quality concerns, and costs to industry.
Huron	Degradation is not as severe as in the lower Great Lakes	Major changes to the food web, fish diseases, and nearshore algal fouling.

Water Quality Impairments

Sections 305(b) and 303(d) of the Clean Water Act require states to report attainment of the water quality goals for their state waterbodies. It is the most comprehensive standardized reporting mechanism for evaluating achievement of "designated use" goals for water quality. According to the most recent data available,[2] 934.8 thousand miles of rivers and streams have been assessed in the last round of reporting (approximately 26 percent of all such waters in the United States). Of those assessed, 464.7 thousand miles (nearly 50 percent) were designated as "good," 463.7 thousand miles, (nearly 50 percent) as "impaired," and 6.4 thousand miles (1 percent) as "threatened." For lakes, reservoirs, and ponds, 17.6 million acres were assessed, with 5.9 million acres (34 percent) rated as "good," 11.6 million acres (66 percent) "impaired," and 47.3 thousand acres as "threatened."

---

[2] http://iaspub.epa.gov/waters10/attains_nation_cy.control, October 30, 2010

On a national level, the probable sources contributing to these impairments (Table 8) are led by agricultural activities (104.3 thousand stream miles and 1.6 million lake acres) and atmospheric deposition (64.1 thousand stream miles, 3.8 million lake acres, and 56.2 thousand mi^2 of open water in the Great Lakes). The combined effects of activities associated with urbanization (for example, urban runoff, municipal discharge, industrial activities, construction, etc.) are also significant causative factors behind the water quality impairments. Although all of these activities impact aquatic ecosystem health, urbanization is known to dramatically impact the condition of fish communities and is highlighted in an associated case study in this report [see Case Study 1: Impacts of Urbanization on Fisheries and Aquatic Ecosystems].

Table 8—EPA National Summary of probable causes of water quality impairment (USEPA http://iaspub.epa.gov/waters10/attains_nation_cy.control, October 12, 2010).

Probable source group	Rivers and streams (mi)	Lakes, reservoirs, and ponds (ac)	Bays and estuaries (mi²)	Coastal shoreline (mi)	Ocean and near coastal (mi²)	Wetlands (acres)	Great Lakes shoreline (mi)	Great Lakes open water (mi²)
Agriculture	104,321	1,579,540	2,885	84	1	383,822		4,373
Aquaculture	1,055	4,490	0					
Atmospheric deposition	64,119	3,772,737	4,238		70	200,741	285	56,254
Commercial harbor activities		109,240	481	20	1			
Construction	12,638	305,080	16	3	3	13,971		
Groundwater loadings/ withdrawals	181	98,009	158			3,045		
Habitat alterations (not directly related to hydromodification)	33,012	359,247	2,091			8,017		
Hydromodification	60,075	1,240,807	2,532		5	115,704		
Industrial	9,924	209,500	3,044	37	3	195,980		3
Land application/waste Sites/tanks	8,003	80,284	52	1		1,634		
Legacy/historical Pollutants	4,191	755,219	254	8			682	15,128
Military bases	42	2						
Municipal Discharges/sewage	38,184	644,660	4,499	107	10	458	27	3
Natural/wildlife	54,403	1,321,007	3,789	100	0	133,558	0	
Other	8,560	777,527	2,406	34		65,874		25
Recreation and tourism (non-boating)	1,668	108,069	0	20	4	787		
Recreational boating and marinas	147	126,174	545	1	8			
Resource extraction	25,489	509,934	582	12		89,353		
Silviculture (forestry)	19,409	247,865	0			2		
Spills/dumping	1,698	176,699	26	13	2			
Unknown	78,419	2,609,586	3,977	13	283	210,159	134	554
Unspecified nonpoint source	44,338	815,722	1,773	106	4	63,901	9	3
Urban-related Runoff/stormwater	32,062	716,410	1,994	47	4	2	2	13,867

Fish Contaminant Advisories

The number of advisories for fish consumption that are issued by state, tribal, and federal governments cannot be used to indicate trends in the conditions of the waters of the United States. The variability in criteria for issuing advisories, monitoring, and other data collection among the agencies responsible for issuing advisories creates inconsistencies that do not allow the establishment of national trends in fish advisories (USEPA 2009). Additionally, continually advancing technologies that allow for the detection of smaller levels of contaminants, greater focus on sampling programs over time, and other factors make year-to-year comparisons inaccurate.

Despite their lack of utility for assessing trends, advisories can be one piece of a gross snapshot of water quality. By themselves, they should not be used as an absolute indicator of water condition. A summary is provided here as simply an indication of the status of fish consumption advisories in the United States in 2008.

All 50 states, the District of Columbia, the territories of American Samoa and Guam, and five Native American tribes have issued fish consumption advisories. There are currently 4,249 advisories in place, an increase of 397 since the previous reporting period in 2006. These advisories cover 18 million lake acres and 1.4 million river miles (an increase of 18 percent, and 52 percent respectively since 2006) representing 43 percent of the total lake acreage and 39 percent of the river miles of the United States. However, this increase is not necessarily due to additional degradation of the waterways; it is attributed primarily to the issuance of several new advisories covering entire states instead of specific water bodies (USEPA 2009).

Advisories have been issued covering 34 different chemical contaminants. Ninety-seven percent of all advisories involve only five bioaccumulative chemical contaminants: mercury, polychlorinated biphenyls (PCBs), chlordane, dioxins, and dichlorodiphenyltrichloroethane (DDT) (Table 9).

Table 9—Number of advisories, lake acres, and river miles under fish consumption advisories for five major contaminants in the United States in 2008 (from USEPA 2009).

Chemical	Number of advisories	Lake area under advisory (ac)	River length under advisory (mi)
Mercury	3,361	16,808,032	1,254,893
PCBs	1,025	6,049,506	130,248
Chlordane	67	842,913	54,029
Dioxins	123	35,400	2,055
DDT	76	876,520	69,198

Fish Populations

To understand the situation of assessing status and trends of fisheries and aquatic resources, one must understand the fundamental basis for management of these resources in the United States. With only a few exceptions, responsibility for managing freshwater and near-shore marine fisheries resides with state and, in some cases, Native American tribal, governments. Exceptions exist for federal "trust" species which generally are threatened species, endangered species, interjurisdictional fish, marine mammals, and other species of concern, where the federal government's role varies depending on status of a particular species.

With rare exception (for example, certain federal trust species), analysis of the status and trends of freshwater fisheries is conducted independently by individual states. Sampling programs, collection methodologies, and data protocols are developed by each state to meet their individual needs. Historic management approaches have focused on a waterbody-by-waterbody basis, not a statewide or ecosystem management basis. This system of management, which tends to work well for local fisheries management by individual states, does not lend itself to conducting large scale (regional or national) analyses of status and trends of freshwater aquatic populations.

In 1998, the U.S. Geological Survey's Biological Resources Discipline conducted a comprehensive assessment of United States resources on a region-by-region basis. The USGS effort, which included fisheries and aquatic resources, engaged an extensive network of professionals from within the USGS ranks, universities, and other agencies. While the resulting report documents many case-by-case examples of the trends in specific fish populations, it falls short of a comprehensive analysis of the status and trends of aquatic species that is representative of an entire nation or region. The report noted that:

> "Substantial trend information is only found on birds, some game animals, and commercially exploited species. And much of the information concerning exploited species comes from the harvest activity itself and is not independently measured. Thus, the limited information itself sometimes reflects the biases and limitations of the practitioners" (Mac and others 1998, vol 1:4).

This underscores the findings of previous RPA assessments (Flather and Hoekstra 1989; Loftus and Flather 2000), that information is substantially lacking, particularly in the freshwater environment, to conduct a comprehensive status and trends analysis.

However, in recent decades, increasing coordination among agencies in collection methods (Bonar and others 2009) and coordinated systems to report information (Loftus and Beard 2009; Beard and others 1998) are improving the ability to utilize fisheries data that are collected by disparate agencies to develop regional status and trends analyses. Until these systems are more developed, a comprehensive status and trends of freshwater fisheries analysis will remain elusive. An example application of one of these systems that was initiated in part by the USDA Forest Service, the Multistate Aquatic Resources Information System (MARIS), for developing trend information is found in an accompanying case study [see Case Study 2: Exploring Trends in Largemouth Bass Relative Abundance with MARIS]

Marine and Estuarine Fish Stocks

States also maintain management authority for most near-shore marine species occurring within state waters (generally extending seaward 3 miles from the shoreline). However, a series of interstate fisheries commissions collectively covering all United States coastal waters has improved coordination among the states for management and stock assessment of fish that migrate through multiple state jurisdictions. On the Atlantic coast, while management authority still resides with state governments coordinating management programs through this interstate compact, the federal government maintains a role in helping to enforce the provisions of the management plans. This situation is unique to the Atlantic coast and is not in place on either the Gulf of Mexico or Pacific coasts.

This report highlights a few species that are likely to be impacted by changes in landscape usage due to life history strategies that make them dependent on inland freshwater (or estuarine) habitats. The inclusion or exclusion of species is somewhat arbitrary; at its broadest interpretation nearly all species could be included. The accompanying case study on northwest Pacific salmon highlights one such fishery that is clearly impacted by landscape changes and which the Forest Service plays a key role through management of National Forest system lands [see Case Study 3: Status of Northwest Pacific Salmon].

Diadromous species depend on fresh water for either reproduction or, conversely, in their adult stages and thus are directly impacted by nearshore habitat conditions. Table 10 lists the truly diadromous species on the East coast that are covered under management plans of the Atlantic States Marine Fisheries Commission (horseshoe crabs are included due to their direct dependence on beaches for reproduction). Of these, only Atlantic striped bass populations are considered to be healthy although concern is increasing due to downward trends in key population metrics [see Case Study 4: Atlantic Coast Striped Bass].

Table 10—Status and trends of select Atlantic coast nearshore species considered to be diadromous and covered by interstate fishery management plans (source: Atlantic States Marine Fisheries Commission, www.asmfc.org)

Species	Condition
American eel	Unknown; recreational and commercial landings declining.
Atlantic sturgeon	Overfished; proposed for listing under Endangered Species Act.
Horseshoe crab	Unknown; declines in commercial harvest; increasing trends in abundance in the southeast and Delaware Bay regions and decreasing abundance in the New York and New England regions.
American shad	Most stocks have significantly declined from historic levels and do not appear to be recovering.
Striped bass	Healthy; not overfished and overfishing is not occurring; some disease concerns.

Marine species fall outside of the primary focus of the RPA analysis and are only briefly addressed here. The National Marine Fisheries Service (NMFS, also referred to as NOAA Fisheries), a division of the National Oceanic and Atmospheric Administration, is the primary federal agency responsible for managing fisheries and fish stocks occurring in the United States' Exclusive Economic Zone (or EEZ, which generally extends from 3 miles to 200 miles offshore). NMFS management occurs through a series of regional management councils and, in some cases, international agreement for highly migratory species. Data collection has tended to focus on those species of high economic or social importance (NMFS 2009a).

For 2009, NMFS reviewed the status of 522 individual stocks and stock complexes. Data was sufficient for 253 of these stocks to make a determination of "overfished and/or overfishing."[3]

---

[3] A stock that is subject to overfishing has a fishing mortality (harvest) rate above the level that provides for the maximum sustainable yield. A stock that is overfished has a biomass level below a biological threshold specified in its fishery management plan.

Forty-six of these stocks (23 percent) were deemed to be overfished and 41 (15 percent) subject to overfishing (NMFS 2010b). This is comparable to 2008, when 46 (23 percent) were overfished and 41 (16 percent) of the stocks with sufficient data were subject to overfishing (Table 11). Four stocks of fish have been rebuilt.

To measure the sustainability of fisheries, NMFS has developed the Fish Stock Sustainability Index (FSSI). This measures the "performance of 230 key stocks that are important to the recreational and commercial fisheries. The FSSI increases as overfishing is ended and stocks rebuild to the level that provides maximum sustainable yield" (the highest yield that can be taken from a fish stock while maintaining a stable population over time) (NMFS 2009b). Stocks with biomass exceeding 80 percent of the level that would produce maximum sustainable yield are considered to be in the "sustainable" range.

Table 11—Status of marine fish stocks (NMFS 2008, 2009, 2010b).

Year	Number of stocks reviewed	Number of stocks with sufficient data	Number of stocks overfished (status)	Number of stocks subject to overfishing (trend)
2007	528	255	45	41
2008	531	259	46	41
2009	522	253	46	38

The FSSI is calculated by assigning a score for each of five attributes of individual fish stocks:

		Maximum Points
1.	"Overfished" status is known.	0.5
2.	"Overfishing" status is known.	0.5
3.	Overfishing is not occurring (for stocks with known "overfishing" status).	1.0
4.	Stock biomass is above the "overfished" level defined for the stock.	1.0
5.	Stock biomass is at or above 80 percent of the biomass that produces maximum sustainable yield (BMSY). This point is in addition to the point awarded for being above the "overfished" level.	1.0

The maximum score that each stock may receive is 4, which indicates a fish stock in favorable condition. The value of the FSSI is the sum of all 230 individual stock scores. The maximum total FSSI score is 920, achieved if all 230 stocks were to each receive a score of 4.[4] Thus, higher indexes indicate generally increasing sustainability of fisheries (even though some individual fish stocks may be declining while others are increasing). The FSSI increased from 357.5 in 2000 to 573 in 2009 (Figure 5). Since 2000, the FSSI has increased 60 percent indicating a generally improving condition.

---

[4] National Marine Fisheries Service http://www.nmfs.noaa.gov/sfa/statusoffisheries/2010/fourth/Q4%20 2010%20FSSI%20Summary%20Changes.pdf

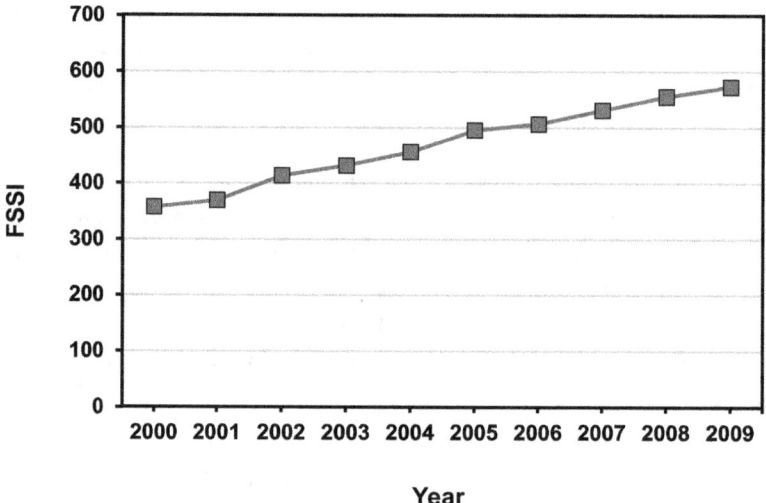

Figure 5—Fish Stock Sustainability Index (FSSI) of 230 key marine fish stocks as determined by NMFS (source: http://www nmfs noaa.gov/sfa/statusoffisheries/2010/first/q1_2010_fssi_summary_changes.pdf).

Species of Conservation Concern

Trends in species imperilment can be an indicator of aquatic system health. Currently, a total of 139 species of fish are formally listed as threatened (66 species) or endangered (73 species) under the Endangered Species Act of 1973 (ESA; P.L. 93-205, 87 Stat. 884, as amended; 16 U.S.C. 1531-1536, 1538-1540). Of these, the NMFS leads the recovery of 22 endangered and seven threatened fish species. In addition, 104 endangered and 22 threatened clams, snails, and aquatic crustaceans are on the list (USFWS species listing November 1, 2010).[5] Geographically, formally listed freshwater fish are concentrated in the southern Appalachians, the arid Southwest, and the Pacific Northwest (Figure 6a). The geographic occurrence of all aquatic vertebrates and invertebrates show a similar pattern of concentration, but with notable numbers of listed species occurring in Peninsular Florida and in tributaries associated with the Washbash River in Indiana (Figure 6b).

Perhaps the most comprehensive listing of fishes that are in jeopardy of becoming endangered or extinct is provided by Jelks and others (2008) since it builds from a comparative database over a period of more than 25 years. Collectively termed "imperiled species," the conservation status of each taxon was determined by a panel of experts from the Endangered Species Committee of the American Fisheries Society. The 2008 analysis built from the results of two earlier works of similar nature (Deacon and others 1979 and Williams and others 1989) allowing a comparison of trends in the listing status over that 20 year period.

---

[5] http://www fws.gov/endangered/species/us-species html

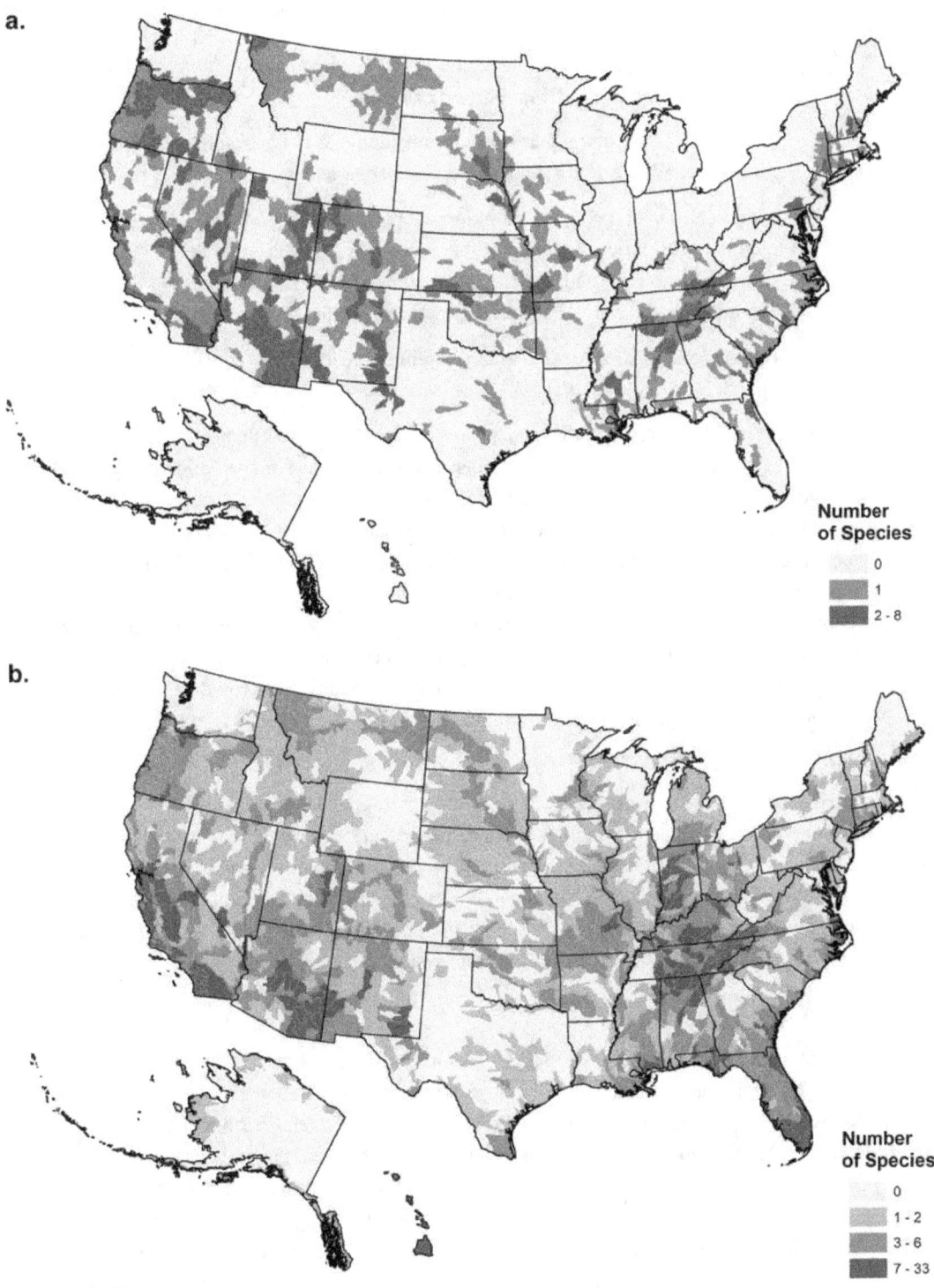

Figure 6—The number of threatened and endangered (a) freshwater fish and (b) aquatic species by 8-digit hydrologic unit for the United States (NatureServe 2010).

The conservation status categories as defined by Jelks and others (2008:374-375) were:

> "Endangered (E): a taxon that is in imminent danger of extinction throughout all or extirpation from a significant portion of its range.
>
> Threatened (T): a taxon that is in imminent danger of becoming endangered throughout all or a significant portion of its range.
>
> Vulnerable (V): a taxon that is in imminent danger of becoming threatened throughout all or a significant portion of its range. This status is equivalent to "Special Concern" as designated by Deacon and others (1979), Williams and others (1989), and many governmental agencies and nongovernmental organizations.
>
> Extinct (X): a taxon of which no living individual has been documented in its natural habitat for 50 or more years."

For the purposes of this report, the data as presented in Jelks and others (2008) were sorted by RPA region and an analysis of the number of species in each conservation category was conducted. Since the source data were presented on a state-by-state basis, this required removing duplicate species entries that occurred in more than one state in each region. In doing so, named subspecies was used as the lowest classification unit. Therefore, some of the unique but unnamed strains or "distinct population segments" that may appear as separate taxon in Jelks and others (2008) are combined into the larger category of species or subspecies (as appropriate) in our regional analysis. Since a species or subspecies may occur in more than one RPA region, the results of each RPA region are not additive to provide a national picture. Rather, a nationwide summary as reported by Jelks and others (2008) is provided for this purpose (Figure 7a and 7b).

In cases where unnamed strains, distinct population segments, or subspecies (for purposes of the species analysis) were combined but had a different conservation status, the most conservative classification was used. For example, if three strains, each being classified respectively as Vulnerable, Threatened, and Endangered, were combined into a single species, that species was assigned as "Endangered" for this analysis. The classification of "Extinct" was only used if all taxonomic units that were combined were extinct.

Nationwide Status

The most recent compilation from Jelks and others (2008) includes 700 taxa in total (all taxa including strains and unnamed distinct populations). Nearly 40 percent of North American freshwater fish species (including the United States, Canada, and northern Mexico) are imperiled (Figure 7). In 2008, 230 were classified as vulnerable, 190 threatened, 280 endangered, and 61 presumed extinct. This is a 92 percent and 179 percent increase over the taxa listed by Williams and others (1989) and Deacon and others (1979), respectively. However, a more comprehensive source list used by Jelks and others may be attributable to at least a portion of this increase. Jelks and others (2008:382) reported that "…the pronounced increase primarily results from the addition of taxa that became imperiled since 1989, recent discoveries of nominal and undescribed taxa regarded as imperiled, newly added distinct populations, and inclusion of extinct taxa." They also note that only 8 (2 percent) of the taxa listed in 1989 improved sufficiently to be delisted; 91 percent remained the same or declined.

a.

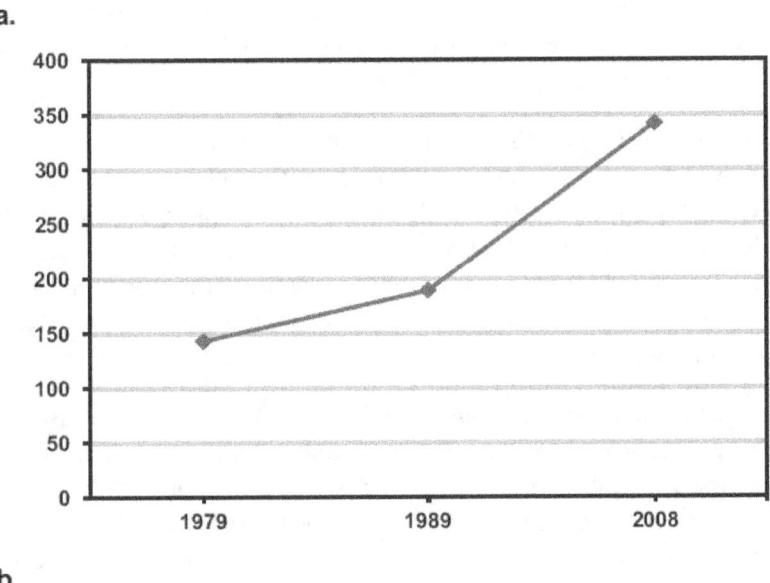

b.

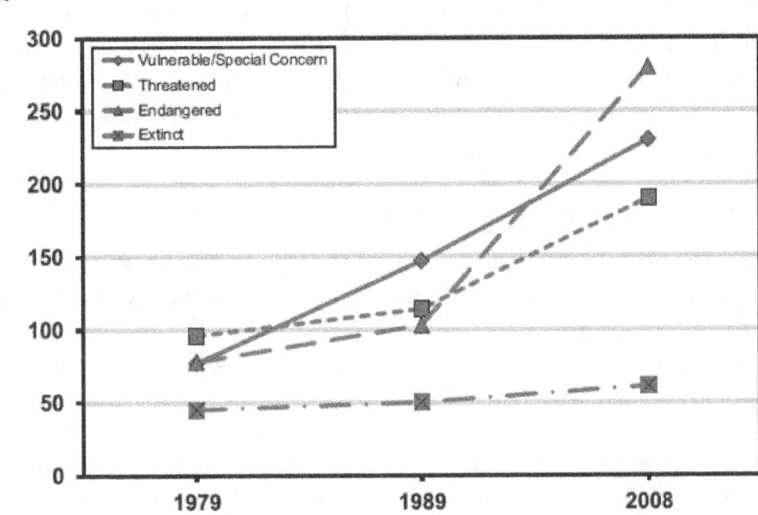

Figure 7 –Number of fish (a) species considered to be vulnerable, threatened, endangered, or extinct and (b) subspecies by each classification (Jelks and others 2008).

In assembling the list of imperiled taxa, Jelks and others also identified the causative factors contributing to the conservation status similar to that used by Deacon (1979) and Williams (1989). These factors included: destruction, modification, or reduction of habitat; over-exploitation or intentional eradication either directly or of an organism on which the taxa relied for some part of its survival; disease or parasitism; a narrowly restricted range; and other factors, including impacts of nonindigenous organisms and hybridization.

Habitat degradation was listed as one of the causative factors on most cases (92 percent) followed by restricted range (72 percent). Thirty-eight percent of the listed taxa had both of these factors as criteria for listing.

Based on the data presented in Jelks and others (2008), three distinct regions within the United States with large numbers of imperiled taxa are the southeastern United States, the mid-Pacific coast, and the lower Rio Grande, similar to what was reported in the last RPA report (Loftus and Flather 2000). Although the incidence of imperilment spread across many taxa, particularly vulnerable were western salmon and trout (where more than 60 percent are considered at risk), darters in the southeastern United States, and pupfish and livebearers in the southwestern United States.

Based on occurrence data obtained from NatureServe (2010), we mapped at-risk species by 8-digit hydrologic units across the coterminous United States. Concentrations of at-risk freshwater fish species (full species only) occur throughout the southeastern United States (Southern Appalachians and scattered watersheds in the Coastal Plain region); the central United States; the arid Southwest; and in a localized set of watersheds associated with the Klamath River on the Oregon/California boarder (Figure 8a). If we broaden the taxonomic groups to include all vertebrate and invertebrate species that are associated with aquatic habitats, then once again areas of concentration emerge in Peninsular Florida, watersheds associated with the Ohio River system, and watersheds associated with the lower Sacramento and San Joaquin River systems (Figure 8b).

Imperiled Species Trends by RPA Region

The four RPA regions are very broad and formed on the basis of state political boundaries. Subsequently, each RPA region can encompass many of the smaller geographic ecoregions used to characterize the imperilment lists compiled by Jelks and others (2008). However, by compiling the data from Jelks and others on the basis of RPA regions, general patterns emerge similar to that of the smaller ecoregions.

Two analyses are presented for each RPA region: 1) Counts in each conservation classification by subspecies, and 2) Counts in each conservation classification by species. The extent of imperilment (based on number of species or subspecies observed) is substantially greater in the southern RPA region than the other regions[6] From 1979 to 1989, the number of species determined to be "vulnerable" or "endangered" sharply increased while the number of those "threatened" remained relatively steady in this region. The number of "endangered" species increased sharply in the Rocky Mountain and Pacific regions. In the northern RPA region, the increase in "vulnerable" species noticeably exceeded the relative stability of the other two categories (Figures 9a–h). The analysis of imperilment was essentially the same at both the species and subspecies levels in the northern RPA region since few taxa in this region were identified below the species level.

---

[6] For purposes of this analysis, species counts from Alaska and Hawaii are not included in the Pacific RPA region since data from those states were not available from Jelks and others (2008).

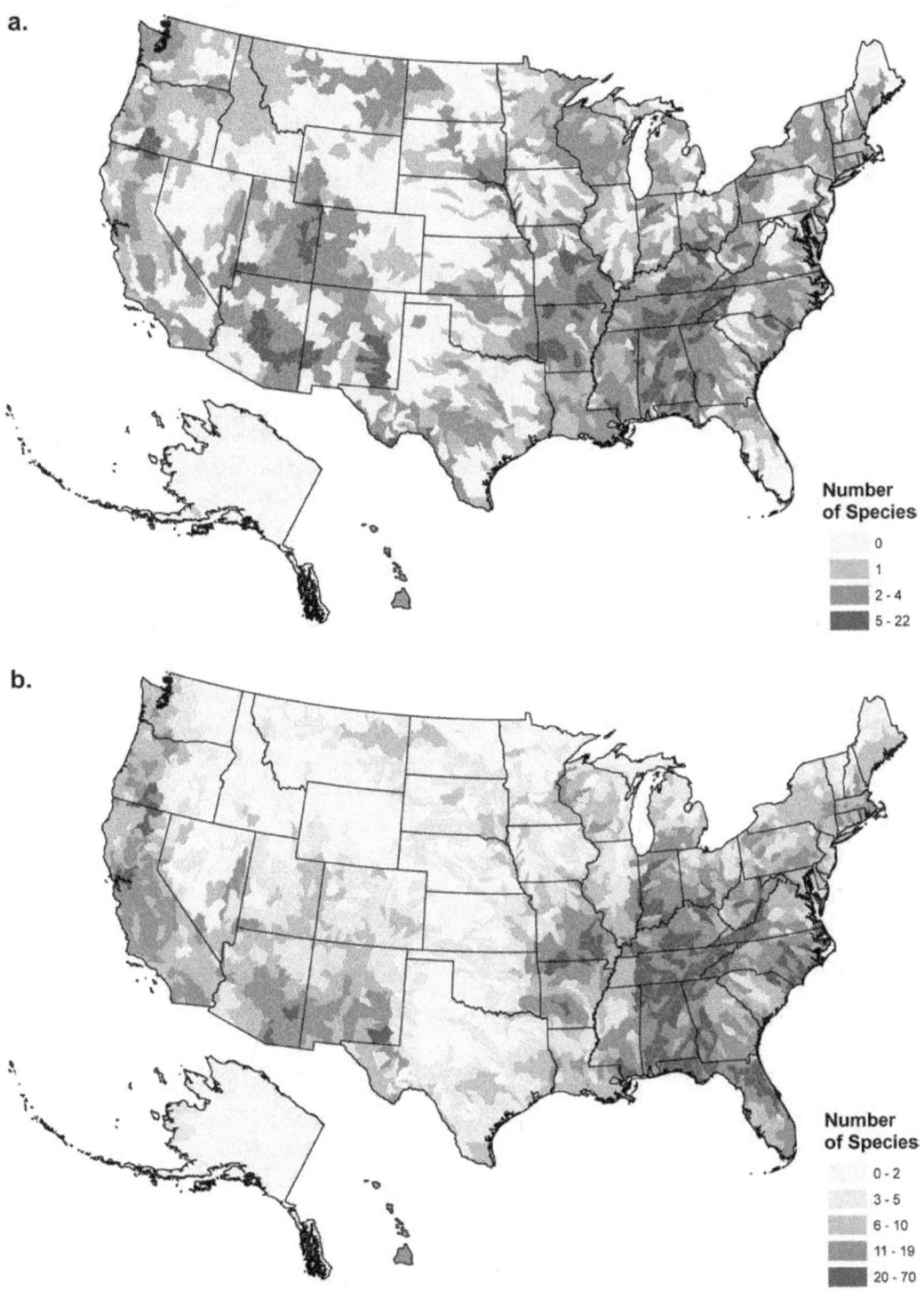

Figure 8—The number of at-risk (a) freshwater fish and (b) aquatic species by 8-digit hydrologic unit for the United States (NatureServe 2010).

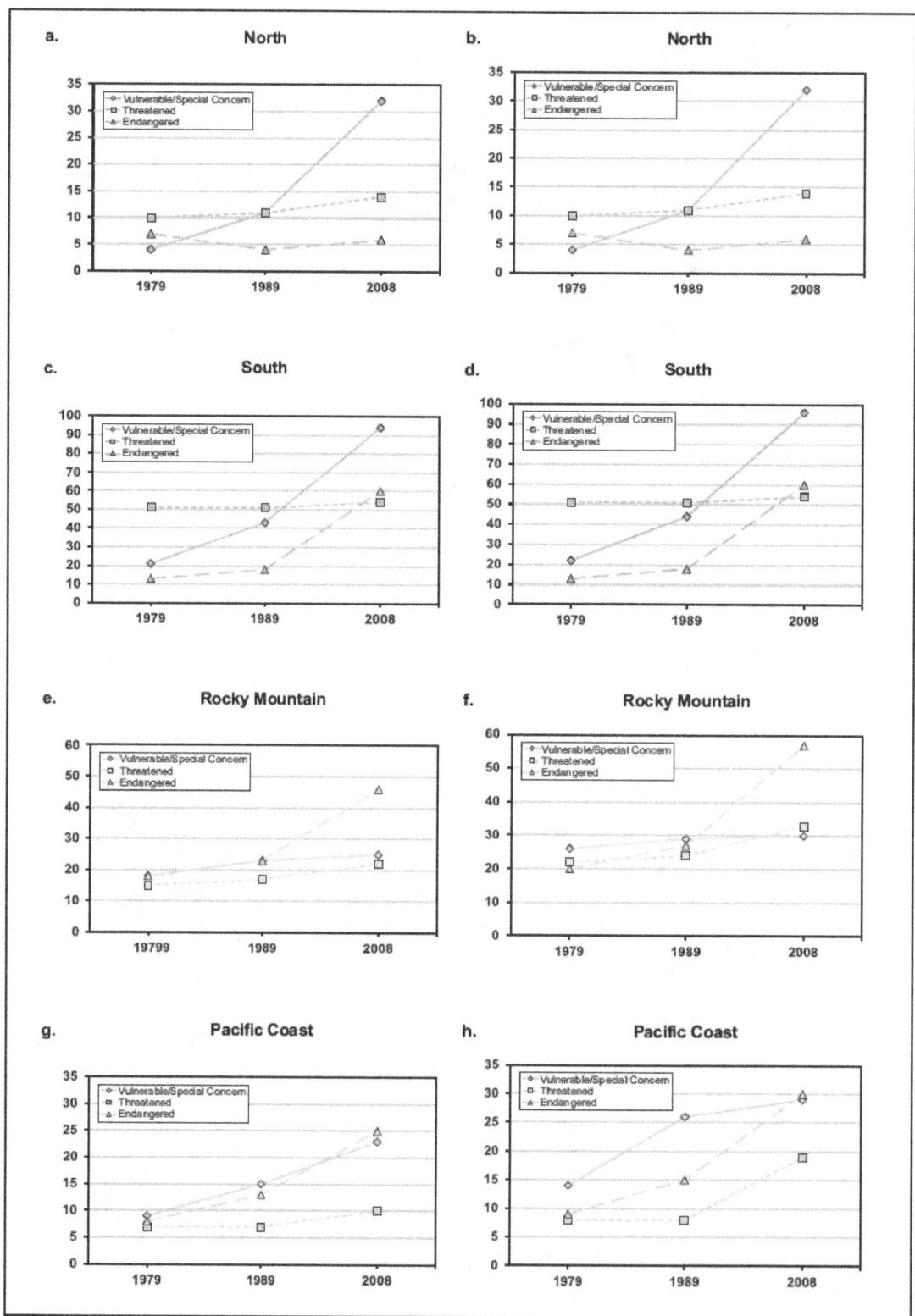

Figure 9—The number of fish considered to be vulnerable, threatened, or endangered by species (a, c, e, g) and subspecies (b, d, f, h) in each RPA region by year (Jelks and others 2008).

Marine Species

NOAA Fisheries is the lead agency responsible for listing marine and anadromous species under the ESA. Currently, 29 marine and anadromous fish, 20 marine mammals (10 whales, 3 dolphins, 1 porpoise, 5 seals, 2 sea lions), 8 sea turtles, 3 marine invertebrates (coral, abalone), and 1 marine plant are covered under the portion of the ESA program that is overseen by NOAA Fisheries.

Trends in Harvest

While the harvest of species is often used as a surrogate for species population status and trends, it must be done so very carefully and nonetheless may still lead to erroneous conclusions (Branch and others 2011). In addition to stock status, a number of other factors influence the amount (numbers or biomass) of species harvested, including fishing effort, gear efficiencies, economics (value) of landed fish (which influences effort), and weather patterns. However, the RPA directs that measures of utilization be included in resource assessments. In addition to the socioeconomic implications, harvest can impact taxonomic and functional diversity of aquatic communities, abundance of species, and genetic diversity of individual populations (Mac and others 1998). Thus, socioeconomics measures are an important aspect of assessing the biological status of aquatic communities.

The total harvest (edible and industrial) of commercial species by fishermen at United States ports in 2008 was 8.3 billion pounds (3.8 million metric tons) valued at $4.4 billion. This was a decrease of 983.4 million pounds (11 percent), continuing a trend of the past three years (Figure 10a), but it was an increase of $191.6 million in ex-vessel value (up 5 percent) compared with the previous year. Finfish (free swimming fish with fins, as opposed to crabs, oysters, etc.) accounted for 87 percent of these landings (Table 12) but only 51 percent of the value. For the past twenty years, landings of Pacific salmon species (Chinook, Coho, Pink, Sockeye, and Chum), which include Pacific Northwest stocks as well as Alaskan stocks, have fluctuated between 600 million and nearly 1 billion pounds annually.

Trends in commercial harvest landed in United States Great Lakes ports continued their decline (Figure 10b).There is now evidence that non-native fishes like Asian carps can have ecosystem-scale effects on the condition of native fish species (Irons and others 2007). Given that more than 180 non-native species have already been detected in the Great Lakes (including sea lamprey, zebra mussel, round goby, spiny waterflea, and Eurasian watermilfoil), there are mounting concerns that colonization of the Great Lakes by Asian carp species will further erode the integrity of the native fish communities and diminish populations of species that are important to recreational and commercial fisheries (International Joint Commission 2011, Rasmussen and others in press).

Outside of the Great Lakes, the harvest of aquatic organisms from freshwater systems of the United States is unknown. Limited commercial fishing occurs in the Great Lakes, Mississippi/Missouri River System, and in some other areas for specific species (for example, snapping turtles in many states). Most freshwater fish are harvested by recreational anglers (see Thayer and Loftus 2012 for specific example). Although effort estimates are available for recreational angling, including anglers targeting specific fish species (discussed later), national or regional harvest estimates are not available. Effort alone is not a reliable indicator of harvest; nationwide, 67 percent of anglers report releasing some fish, 20 percent report releasing all fish that they caught, and 84 percent report releasing fish that they legally could have kept (USDI and USDC 2007).

a.

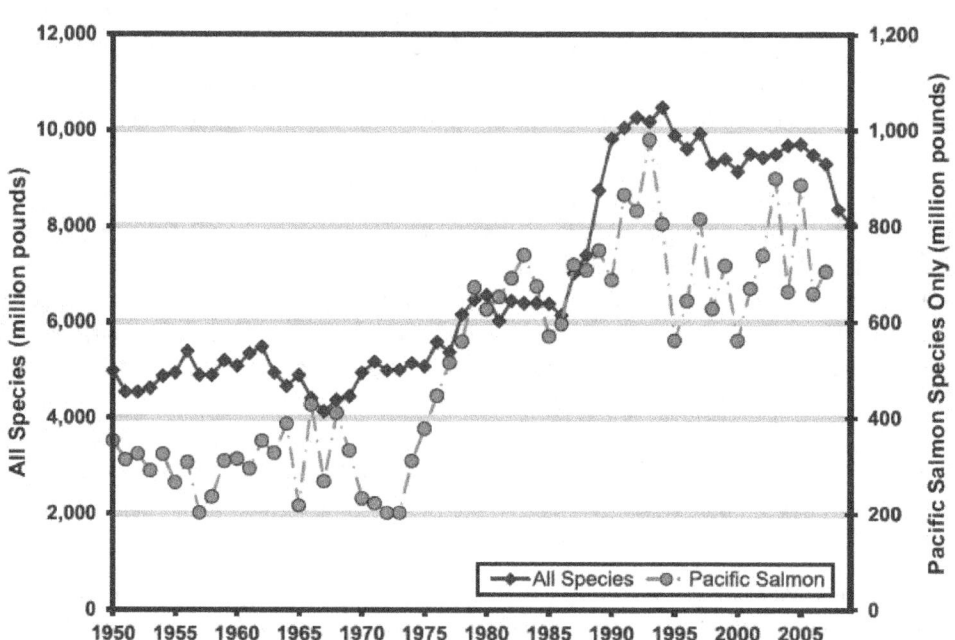

b.

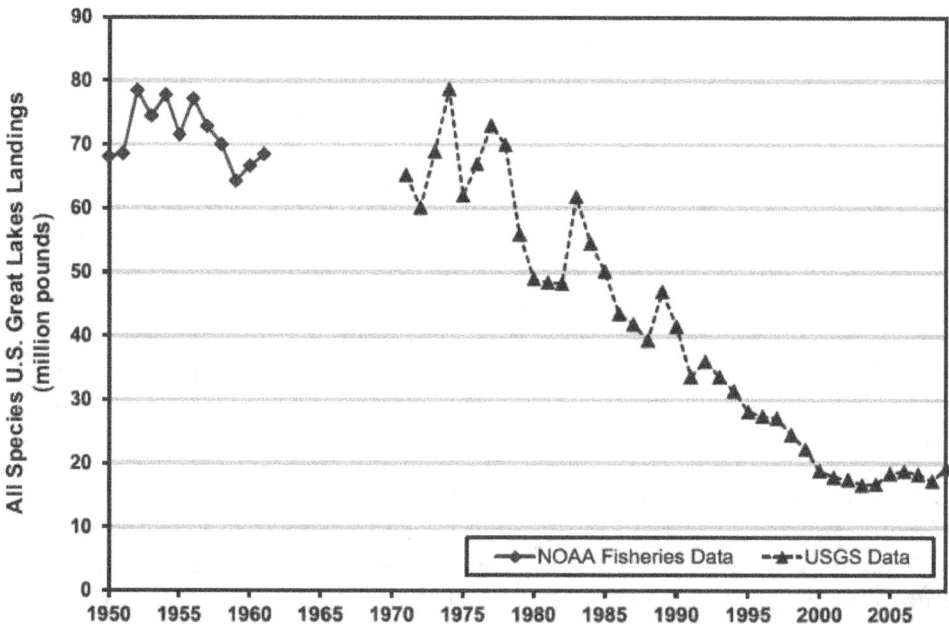

Figure 10 (a) Commercial landings (pounds) of all marine species and Pacific salmon species in United States ports (source: NOAA Fisheries http://www.st.nmfs noaa.gov/st1/commercial/index html October 27, 2011) and (b) all species from U.S. Great Lakes. (source: 1950-1961 NOAA Fisheries; 1971-2009 U.S. Geological Survey Great Lakes Science Center http://www.st nmfs noaa.gov/st1/commercial/land-ings/gl_query.html October 28, 2011; 1962-1970 unavailable).

Table 12—Domestic species landings in 2008 ranked by biomass and value (NMFS 2009a).

	Pounds			Dollars	
Rank	Species	Lbs (x1000)	Rank	Species	US$ (x1000)
1	Pollock	2,298	1	Crabs	562,267
2	Menhaden	1,341	2	Shrimp	441,818
3	Flatfish	663	3	Salmon	394,594
4	Salmon	658	4	Scallops	371,641
5	Hakes	550	5	Lobster	336,902
6	Cod	513	6	Pollock	334,477
7	Crabs	325	7	Cod	304,895
8	Herring (sea)	259	8	Halibut	217,735
9	Shrimp	257	9	Clams	186,718
10	Sardines	193	10	Flatfish	184,209

Trends in Participation

Recreational Fisheries

The primary source of national level recreational fishing information is a survey conducted every five years by the U.S. Fish and Wildlife Service and U.S. Census Bureau. Initiated in 1955, this "National Survey of Fishing, Hunting, and Wildlife Associated Recreation" (herein referred to as the National Survey) has undergone several changes in methodology that limit the comparability of surveys conducted prior to 1991 and those after.

National Participation

Fishing remains the most popular form of outdoor recreation that is dependent upon wildlife and fish. The most recent survey (2006) revealed that 30 million individuals in the United States, or 13 percent of United States population age 16 years and older, participated in recreational fishing within the United States. This was a 12 percent decline from the previous survey in 2001 and a 16 percent decline from 1991 (Figure 11), the earliest year in the comparable time series (USDI and USDC 2007). Anglers spent 517 million days on the water in 2006, a 7 percent decline from 2001, but relatively unchanged since 1991. Within this time series, angler days peaked in 1996 at 626 million days. Despite the substantial declines in recent decades, the number of anglers closely approximates the number in 1980 and is twice as many as in 1955 based on a standardized index of participation (Richard Aiken, U.S. Fish and Wildlife Service, personal communication). Excluding Great Lakes anglers, 72 percent of the days spent fishing in freshwater were on lakes, reservoirs, and ponds and 32 percent on freshwater rivers and streams.[7] The favored species sought by these anglers were smallmouth/largemouth bass, panfish, and catfish/bullheads (Table 13) (USDI and USDC 2007).

---

[7] Note: Percentages sum to more than 100 due to multiple responses.

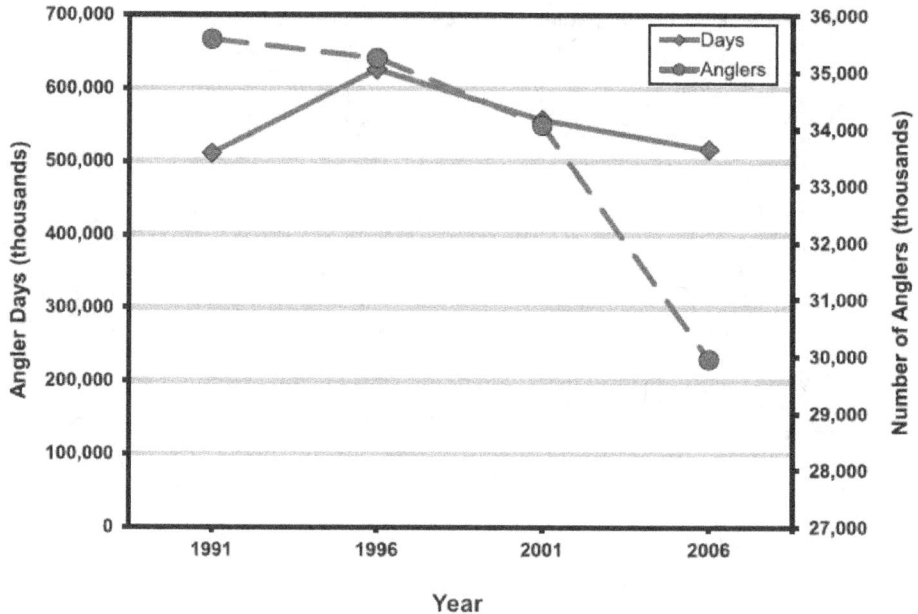

Figure 11—Number of anglers and days spent fishing in the United States 1991-2006 (USDI and USDC 2007).

Table 13—Top freshwater (excluding Great Lakes) species sought by anglers in the United States (USDI and USDC 2007).

Species	Days of fishing (thousands)
Black bass (smallmouth, largemouth, etc.)	161,005
Panfish	101,569
Catfish and bullheads	98,190
Crappie	90,732
Trout	75,485
White bass, striped bass, hybrids	65,211

RPA Regional Statistics

Regional trends for recreational fishing participation generally follow the national level trends. The steepest declines in number of anglers occurred in the Pacific RPA region, with 2001-2006 declines of 24 percent and 1991-2006 declines of 28 percent.[8] The Southern region experienced the smallest loss of number of anglers, declining 7 percent in 2001-2006 and 8 percent in 1991-2006 (Figure 12).

---

[8] Although summing the number of anglers in each state to obtain regional estimates likely over-counts the number of anglers, it can provide an estimate of angling where the activity took place.

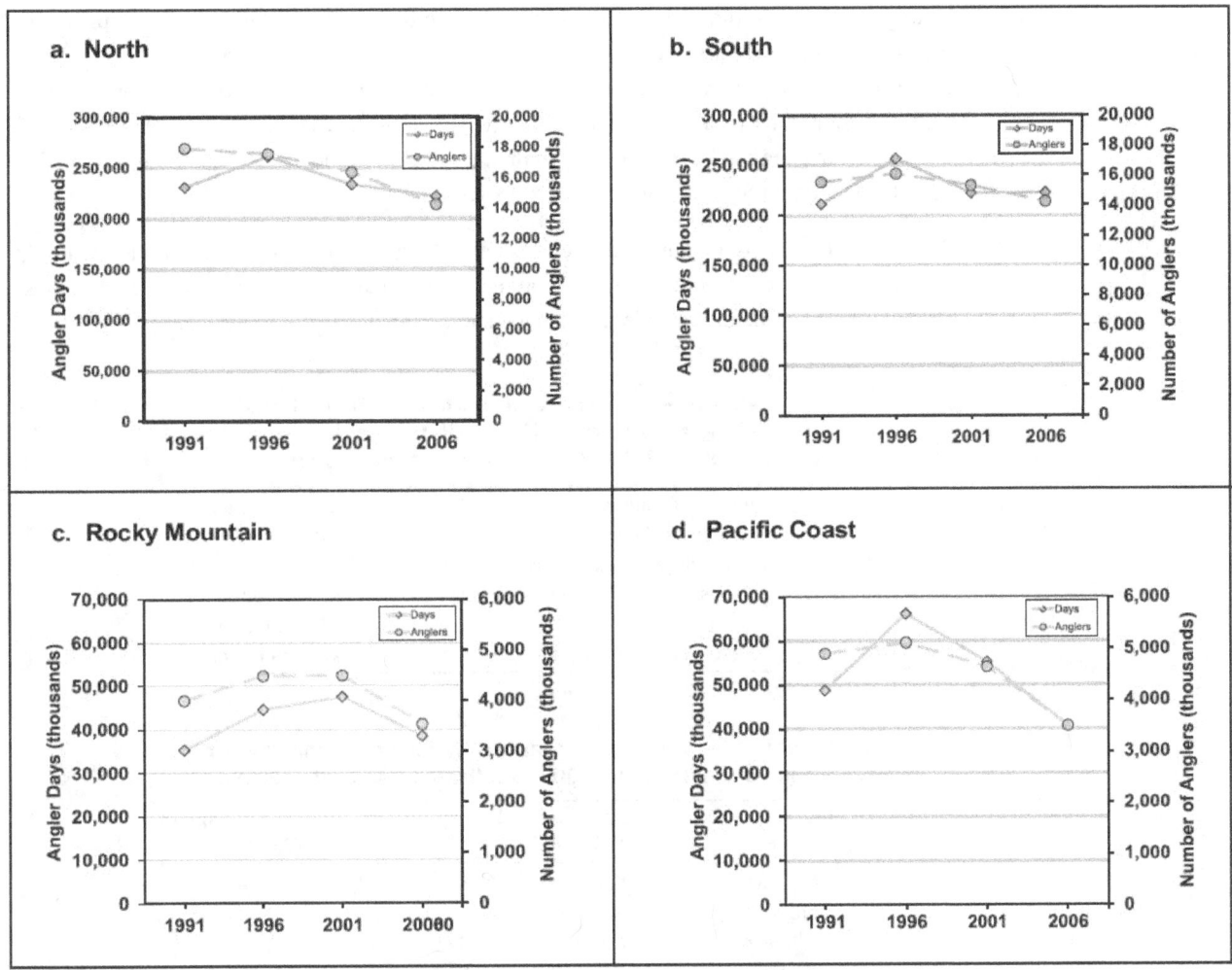

Figure 12—Number of anglers and days spent fishing in the North (a), South (b), Rocky Mountain (c), and Pacific Coast (d) RPA regions from 1991-2006 (USDI and USDC 2007).

In terms of angler days, the pattern of generally declining trends continued, although not as precipitously as the number of anglers. Two regions experienced an overall increase over the longer time span 1991-2006 (Rocky Mountain up 9 percent and South up 1 percent). The Pacific Coast and North regions declined 25 percent and 5 percent, respectively. During the 2001-2006 period, all regions declined in number of angling days, ranging from a 5 percent drop in the North to a 26 percent loss in the Pacific Coast (Figure 12).

Economics of Recreational Fishing

The activity of recreational fishing generates significant economic impact both regionally and nationally. Expenditure estimates collected by the National Survey provide the basis for economic impact analysis of recreational fishing. Using these data, economists have developed economic impact estimates (economic impact, sales, taxes, and jobs) using the IMPLAN economic assessment model from MIG, Inc. (Stillwater, Minnesota).

Nationally, the 30 million anglers age 16 years and older spent $45.3 billion on equipment and trip-related expenses pursuing their sport in the United States during 2006 (Table 14). This translated into an economic impact of more than $124 billion to the national economy associated with more than 1 million jobs. Fishing activity in Florida, Texas, Minnesota, California, and Michigan generated the most, each with more than $2 billion in economic impact attributable to recreational fishing (Table 15) (Southwick Associates 2008).

Regionally, the economic impact of recreational fishing ranged from $7.3 billion in the Rocky Mountain region to $29.3 billion in the South. The South also had the largest number of jobs attributed to the economic activities tied to recreational fishing, with nearly 300,000 (Table 16).

Table 14—Economic contributions of recreational fishing activity in the United States, anglers 16 years and older, 2006 (Southwick Associates 2008).

Number of anglers	29.952 million
Expenditures/retail sales	$45.336 billion
Total multiplier effect (economic output)	$124.959 billion
Salaries, wages and business earnings	$38.360 billion
Jobs	1.036 million
Federal, state and local taxes	$16.359 billion

Table 15—Top 10 states ranked by total expenditures for recreational fishing, 2006 (Southwick Associates 2008).

State	RPA Region	Expenditures (billion)	Number of anglers (million)
Florida	South	$4.412	2.767
Texas	South	$3.367	2.527
Minnesota	North	$2.832	1.427
California	Pacific	$2.677	1.730
Michigan	North	$2.099	1.394
Pennsylvania	North	$1.795	0.994
Wisconsin	North	$1.755	1.394
South Carolina	South	$1.493	0.810
North Carolina	South	$1.204	1.263
Missouri	North	$1.180	1.076

Table 16—Economic impact of recreational fishing activity by RPA region (based on data from Southwick Associates 2008).

Region	Sales (billion)	Total multiplier effect (billion)	Salaries, wages, and business earnings (billion)	Retail jobs (thousand)	Federal tax revenues (billion)	State and local tax revenues (billion)
North	$17.372	$28.693	$8.806	278.9	$2.106	$1.892
Pacific Coast	$4.991	$8.438	$2.725	77.1	$0.629	$0.569
Rocky Mountain	$4.569	$7.355	$2.184	73.1	$0.491	$0.451
South	$17.342	$29.318	$8.660	292.4	$1.981	$1.717
United States[1]	$45.336	$124.959	$38.360	1,035.6	$9.012	$7.347

[1] Sum does not add to total due to some respondents not being able to assign purchases to a single state

Recreational Fishing on Forest Service Lands

A 2007 report documents the economic activity associated with recreational fishing on Forest Service lands for the primary purpose of recreational fishing (American Sportfishing Association 2007). The report quantifies both the state and national economic effects of trips to U.S. Forest Service-managed lands. The estimated visits as reported by the U.S. Forest Service National Visitor Use Monitoring Survey (2000 to 2003 cycle) were matched with the expenditure profiles found in Stynes and White (2006). Expenditures were calculated at two geographic scales: (a) a 50-mile radius within the boundary of each Forest Service unit; and (b) statewide for the state in which the unit was located. Due to a change in data sources and methodologies, the results in this report should not be compared to previous U.S. Forest Service (USFS) economic reports produced by the American Sportfishing Association. Due to its targeted methodology, the USFS data is more accurate for USFS participation.

Anglers annually spent $592 million within 50 miles of USFS units (Table 17). These expenditures supported 14,500 jobs and stimulated $66 million in federal income tax receipts. Wildlife viewers added another $168 million in retail sales annually to the regions surrounding Forest Service units, which in turn supported another 4,700 jobs and nearly $15 million in federal income taxes (American Sportfishing Association 2007).

Marine Recreational Fishing

Although the National Survey provides a comprehensive picture of recreational fishing throughout the United States and breaks down the fishing sectors between freshwater and saltwater angling, a more accurate assessment of marine recreational fishing is likely provided through periodic targeted surveys conducted by the NMFS. The results of the NMFS surveys discussed below, and those of the National Survey discussed previously, cannot be compared due to substantial differences in methodology and target audience.

Since 1979, the National Marine Fisheries Service has conducted the Marine Recreational Fisheries Statistics Survey (MRFSS). The principal objective of this survey is to provide estimates of catch and effort of marine recreational anglers over larger geographic areas (for example, coastwide). However, the demand for statistically valid harvest information within increasingly smaller geographic areas (for example, state level) for specific species has resulted in this survey being used for purposes not originally intended and has also resulted in increases in targeted sampling to obtain sufficient sample sizes for such purposes. Changes in geographic coverage since 1981 make nationwide reporting tenuous, principally due to the absence of Pacific and Gulf coast states from the MRFSS sample in some years. However, since 1996 geographic coverage has been relatively stable (although Texas is still not covered by the survey).

Since 1997, recreational fishing effort (number of anglers and trips taken) peaked in 2007, when 14.2 million anglers took an estimated 88.6 million marine recreational fishing trips. This was an increase of 60 percent and 29 percent respectively over the numbers at the beginning of the time series in 1997. Since the 2006 peak, the number of anglers and trips has dipped slightly but remains significantly higher than the early year of the time series (Figure 13) (NMFS 2007, 2010c). In 2009, marine recreational fishing generated nearly $50 billion in sales accounted for more than 327 thousand full and part time jobs. In comparison, in 2006 (the first year of this comparable time series of data) marine recreational fishing generated 64 percent more in sales ($82 billion) and 63 percent more jobs (533.8 thousand) (NMFS 2010c).

Table 17—National and state-specific economic effects of fishing on U.S. Forest Service units, annual average from 2000-2003 (American Sportfishing Association 2007).

State	State and national level effects of wildlife-based recreation occurring in and around national forest communities[1]			State and national level economic significance of wildlife-based recreation, including trip-related and equipment expenditures[2]		
	Retail sales (thousands)	Jobs (full and part-time)	Federal income tax revenues (thousands)	Retail sales (thousands)	Jobs (full and part-time)	Federal income tax revenues (thousands)
Alabama	$612.2	14	$31.6	$1,751.9	39	$88.0
Alaska	$11,287.1	181	$404.5	$111,024.6	2109	$4,632.1
Arizona	$37,735.6	730	$3,060.4	$196,254.8	3735	$15,549.4
Arkansas	$7,080.2	168	$367.8	$14,721.2	327	$714.0
California	$96,716.8	1718	$9,225.3	$462,056.8	8224	$45,413.4
Colorado	$48,057.7	947	$4,387.9	$210,275.5	4067	$18,735.2
Connecticut	n/a	n/a	n/a	n/a	n/a	n/a
Delaware	n/a	n/a	n/a	n/a	n/a	n/a
Florida	$12,975.8	252	$1,017.0	$62,336.6	1152	$4,606.1
Georgia	$10,699.4	205	$924.1	$22,065.9	413	$1,857.3
Hawaii	n/a	n/a	n/a	n/a	n/a	n/a
Idaho	$25,859.3	586	$1,206.3	$99,042.1	1897	$3,904.4
Illinois	$1,849.5	34	$191.6	$3,765.4	67	$372.7
Indiana	$5,620.9	110	$450.7	$11,266.5	231	$927.7
Iowa	n/a	n/a	n/a	n/a	n/a	n/a
Kansas	$329.4	6	$30.1	$901.1	17	$80.3
Kentucky	$12,412.1	241	$775.7	$29,635.7	585	$1,871.0
Louisiana	$476.1	9	$33.8	$1,288.3	24	$87.9
Maine	$27.1	0	$1.3	$77.5	1	$4.1
Maryland	n/a	n/a	n/a	n/a	n/a	n/a
Massachusetts	n/a	n/a	n/a	n/a	n/a	n/a
Michigan	$6,993.3	129	$557.6	$18,068.6	330	$1,475.7
Minnesota	$50,153.1	994	$4,054.9	$153,085.2	3041	$12,171.1
Mississippi	$9,787.1	203	$465.9	$12,114.8	259	$583.8
Missouri	$1,027.0	18	$70.5	$3,234.5	58	$223.5
Montana	$31,260.4	724	$1,381.3	$115,568.6	2549	$4,839.3
Nebraska	$130.9	3	$6.6	$20,405.6	417	$936.1
Nevada	$3,340.4	50	$244.7	$24,520.2	305	$1,501.4
New Hampshire	$424.9	8	$21.1	$1,214.2	22	$63.8
New Jersey	n/a	n/a	n/a	n/a	n/a	n/a
New Mexico	$8,528.4	180	$508.8	$41,734.4	784	$2,554.3
New York	$115.6	2	$6.3	$236.9	4	$13.5
North Carolina	$16,710.5	342	$1,220.0	$54,603.3	1226	$4,621.1
North Dakota	$227.6	5	$10.1	$879.4	17	$35.3
Ohio	$2,798.7	57	$221.2	$6,015.7	124	$520.5
Oklahoma	$1,441.8	34	$74.8	$2,998.7	67	$147.2
Oregon	$39,579.2	718	$2,594.6	$113,037.0	1,963	$7,023.3
Pennsylvania	$5,311.2	100	$447.1	$8,201.0	154	$658.2
Rhode Island	n/a	n/a	n/a	n/a	n/a	n/a
South Carolina	$4,360.0	90	$327.7	$11,469.4	239	$838.9
South Dakota	$5,274.9	118	$235.9	$19,244.0	416	$826.8
Tennessee	$14,832.3	276	$1,158.1	$25,628.1	529	$2,210.0
Texas	$2,820.6	57	$259.0	$8,940.1	161	$749.9
Utah	$43,396.7	1,006	$2,496.8	$184,460.6	4,146	$10,264.2
Vermont	$5,662.7	90	$309.1	$11,605.7	185	$660.1
Virginia	$19,831.3	368	$1,468.1	$26,843.5	478	$1,927.9
Washington	$18,934.6	347	$1,496.7	$69,020.2	1,175	$5,168.3
West Virginia	$7,179.4	142	$309.4	$9,332.6	178	$388.8
Wisconsin	$7,638.3	161	$381.8	$20,781.2	451	$1,058.7
Wyoming	$12,606.1	232	$427.3	$48,128.8	808	$1,501.1
United States	$592,106.2	14,463	$66,149.6	$2,237,836.2	57,707	$263,938.1

[1] These figures only include expenditures made by people within 50 miles of a USFS unit and generally exclude expenditures for some trip-related and equipment purchased outside the 50 mile radius.

[2] These figures include all trip-related and equipment purchases made within the state and assigned to USFS wildlife-based recreation.

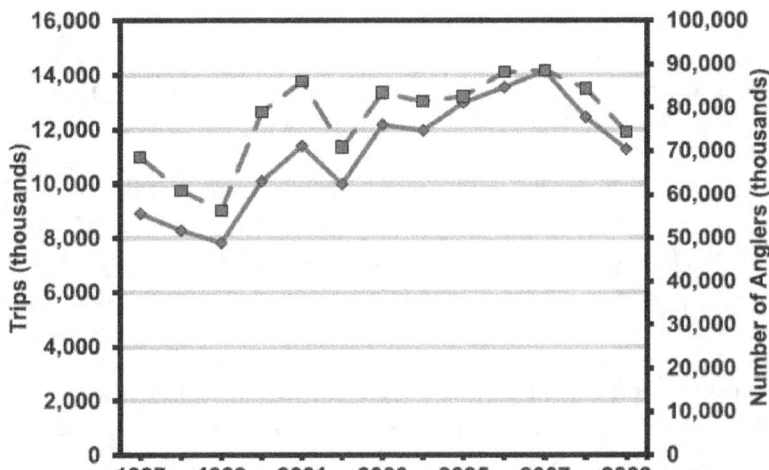

Figure 13—Saltwater recreational anglers and days spent fishing 1997-2008 (NMFS 2007, 2010c).

Commercial Fisheries

From 1965-2001, NMFS compiled the number of commercial fishing craft ("vessels" greater than 5 tons and "boats" less than 5 tons) in the United States. In 2002, such documentation was incomplete and in the following year collection of such information was fully ceased (Dave VanVorhees, NOAA Fisheries, personal communication). No comparable nationwide substitute has been implemented and this information is intended to provide an illustrative completion of a data source that has been included in RPA assessments since 1985. In general, the number of commercial fishing craft has shown a gradual decline since the early 1990s (Figure 14). However, the latter years of the time series may not be comprehensive enough to draw definitive conclusion (Dave Van Vorhees, NOAA Fisheries, personal communication) and reduction in the number of craft alone may not indicate a reduction in fishing effort or harvesting capacity.

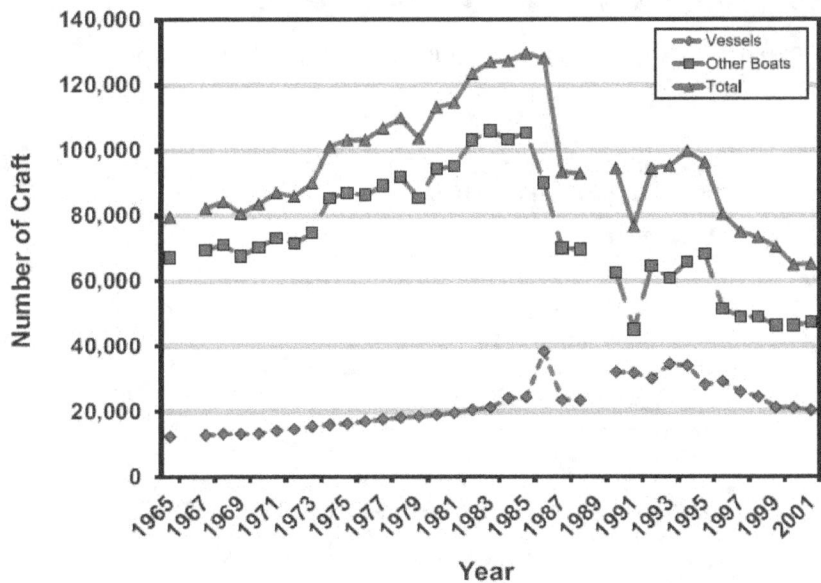

Figure 14—Number of commercial fishing craft registered in the United States (USDI Bureau of Commercial Fisheries [1967-1969]; NMFS [1971-75, 1976a, 1976b, 1977, 1978, 1979, 1980a, 1980b, 1981-83, 1984a, 1984b, 1985-1996]).

In 2009, per capita consumption of fish and shellfish in the United States was 15.8 pounds (edible meat, fresh, frozen, canned, and cured) (NMFS 2010d). This was 0.2 pounds less than consumed in 2008 but still within the highest range observed since the time series began in 1910 (Figure 15).

Beginning in 2006, NMFS has conducted an annual analysis of the economics of marine fisheries. In 2009 the ex-vessel value of edible and industrial landings totaled $3.9 billion (Table 18), a 5 percent decline from 2006 (the first year of the time series). In 2009, commercial fishing in the United States generated more than 1 million full and part time jobs and more than $116 billion in sales.

Overall, the entire commercial seafood industry (harvesters, wholesalers, distributors, processors, dealers, and retailers) generated over $103 billion in sales, $44.3 billion income, and supported 1.5 million jobs in 2006. The commercial harvesting sector alone generated $9.1 billion (9 percent of the total) of the total sales (NMFS 2007).

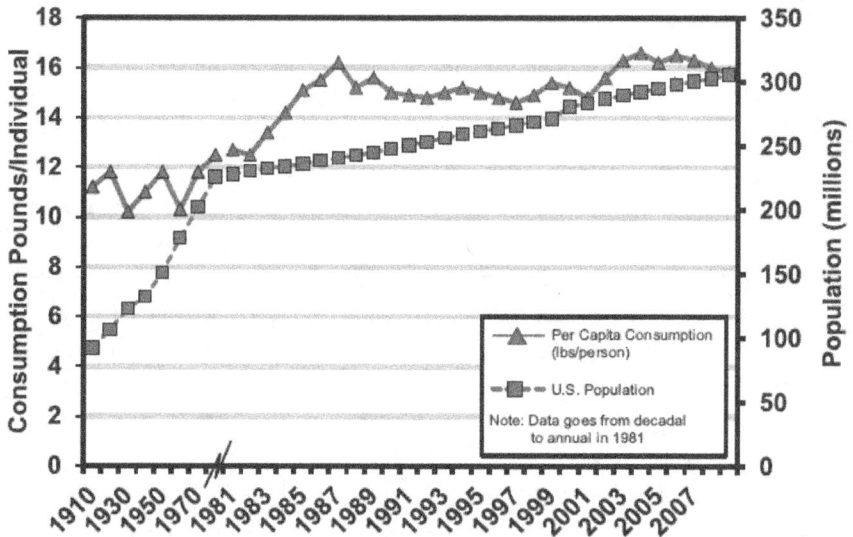

Figure 15—Per capita consumption of fish and shellfish in the United States (NMFS 2010d).

Table 18—U.S. Commercial Fishery Statistics, 2009 (NMFS 2010c).

Total species	
Total landings	7.9 billion pounds
Ex-vessel price	$3.9 billion
Sales (all sectors)	$116 billion
Income (all sectors)	$31.6 billion
Top 5 revenue generators	
Shrimp	$378 million
Sea scallops	$376 million
Pacific salmon	$370 million
Walleye pollock	$308 million
American lobster	$303 million

Management Implications

Data Availability

Since publication of the first RPA assessment (USDA, Forest Service 1977), the data needed to conduct a thorough evaluation of fisheries and aquatic resources has slowly improved. As highlighted in this report, comprehensive aquatic habitat and water quality data is now readily available; a nationwide assessment of the condition of freshwater streams and lakes has been conducted (which establishes an important baseline of information for future assessments); socioeconomic data for extractive use is widely available (some specific to Forest Service lands); and regional information sharing efforts are underway to facilitate the compilation and exchange of fisheries information. Most of these gains have benefited from new electronic technologies that not only allow the rapid distribution of data but also improve the ability to better coordinate sampling and data collection in the field.

Despite these incremental improvements, data remain sorely lacking for a comprehensive assessment of the status and trends of most aquatic biota, including fish that contribute many benefits to human society. This has been noted in previous RPA reports (Loftus and Flather 2000) as well as by other efforts to document status and trends (Mac and others 1998). Positive strides have been made to this end – most noticeably where jurisdictions share management authority over a common stock such as on the Atlantic coast, or where stocks have become severely depleted such as Pacific Northwest salmon. On a limited basis in freshwater systems, states have developed cooperative arrangements for the assessment and management of stocks such as Lake Erie yellow perch and walleye. Still, the ability to assess the status and trends of a single species or species complex nationwide remains elusive. This inability hinders the evaluation of large scale factors that may be impacting aquatic populations across Forest Service regions or across the nation, such as climate change [see Case Study 5: Synopsis of Climate Change Effects on Aquatic Systems], invasive species, or pollution. This in turn impacts the ability to conduct large scale program planning efforts such as may be required by the Forest Service and other agencies.

The 2000 RPA assessment concluded that "data needed to complete a comprehensive assessment of the status and trends of freshwater species in the United States are currently not accessible" (Loftus and Flather 2000: 38). While this is still largely true, programs are underway to improve the situation. The issue lies largely with the accessibility of data, not with the existence of data. Each year, states collect data that could be applied to a status and trends effort. State water quality monitoring efforts as well as state natural resources agencies collect data on fish populations, benthic communities, and water quality. Some of these data have been shown to be applicable for trend analysis (Loftus and Flather 2000; Nate and Loftus this publication, see Case Study 2). Increasingly, states are standardizing the way in which these data are collected, stored, and reported as compared to the past (Loftus 2006). Additionally, multiple federal agencies, including the Forest Service, collect data throughout the United States that could be applied to the assessment of status and trends of aquatic species. Some of these federal programs (for example, National Water-Quality Assessment Program, U.S. Fish and Wildlife Service Fisheries Information System) can be applied to select analysis of metrics that may indicate status and trends, but not in a comprehensive way. The issue becomes one of providing access to data from many of these sources to facilitate comprehensive analysis.

With program funds limited and likely to be so for the near future, avenues need to be developed for leveraging existing projects to achieve gains at multiple geographic and programmatic scales. While the MARIS (described in Case Study 2) embodies this approach for data sharing, a system for addressing fishery and aquatic resource national priorities by leveraging multiple smaller scale projects is described by Hasler and others (2011). Through this system, a network of projects is organized under a single national goal and funding supports these individual projects through a strategic grant program specifically designed to achieve the goal.

The National Fish Habitat Action Plan (NFHAP) is a cooperative program between state and federal agencies, tribal governments, private and NGO partners, and others to address problems impacting fish habitat throughout the United States [see Case Study 6: National Fish Habitat Assessment]. As part of NFHAP, a national data infrastructure has been adopted to exchange data from disparate sources (including state and federal data sources) for multiple purposes. Ultimately, this program may support the development of future national fish habitat assessments that incorporate comprehensive fisheries data. If this system is fully implemented as planned, it will provide a strong basis for future RPA assessments of fisheries and aquatic resources.

Program Planning

Several of the case studies included in this report are directly applicable to Forest Service program planning, including the aforementioned NFHAP Data System. As a cooperator in the NFHAP initiative, the Forest Service can work to ensure the implementation of this system and investigate mechanisms through which data collected as part of Forest Service programs can contribute to this system. In this way, those data collected on Forest Service lands will be represented and influential in future plans for fisheries habitat restoration and evaluation of the long term success of habitat protection and restoration efforts.

The Forest Service manages 193 million acres of forest and grasslands, which contain 128,000 miles of stream, 2.2 million acres of lakes, ponds, and reservoirs, and over 12,000 miles of coastal shoreline (Loftus and Flather 2000). As such, the Forest Service is poised to be a key player in addressing large scale changes to fisheries and aquatic ecosystems stemming from such broad-scale threats as climate change, invasive species, and water quality degradation.

Several projects are already ongoing within the Forest Service to research and evaluate potential courses of action to take in response to climate change. Rieman and Isaak (2010) have suggested many actions, some of which are outlined in the accompanying case study [see Case Study 5: Synopsis of Climate Change Effects on Aquatic Systems], that include conserving and expanding critical habitat for species susceptible to the impacts of climate change (particularly increasing water temperature, and sedimentation); establishing refuge zones to preserve these species; reducing non-climate stresses, particularly those known to impact aquatic systems on Forest Service lands; coordinating efforts among program areas and other agencies; and reinforcing connectivity of stream systems through actions such as retrofitting dysfunctional road culverts and evaluating the utility of removing other artificial barriers to fish movements. With such large areas of water and land under Forest Service management, actions taken by the agency, particularly if implemented in concert with plans by state and other federal agencies, can produce measurable improvements in the future condition of fisheries and aquatic resources.

Forest Service lands can also be a buffer to the deleterious impacts of urbanization on aquatic systems. The effects of urbanization begin with the cutting of roads to allow access to previously undeveloped land and increase with additional fracturing of the landscape. Large tracts of undeveloped lands (undeveloped for either agriculture or urban development) in the National Forest System provide areas where the influences of development on aquatic systems are minimized (but see Radeloff and others 2010). Even National Forest lands that are located in more urban settings can play an important role in protecting aquatic health. As documented in the accompanying case study [see Case Study 1: Impacts of Urbanization on Fisheries and Aquatic Ecosystems], research indicates that maintaining contiguous undeveloped buffers along waterways is significantly more effective than a fractured buffer system.

Case Study 1: Impacts of Urbanization on Fisheries and Aquatic Ecosystems _____

By their very nature, aquatic systems are recipients of the products of activities on the surrounding landscape. Wetlands, streams, and lotic waters are recipients of the runoff from the watershed and transporters of that runoff to waters at lower geographic elevations. The same anthropogenic processes that affect terrestrial species by reducing landscape connectivity, habitat availability, and increasing patch diversity can have a quantifiable effect on aquatic assemblage structure (Kennen and others 2005). In short, the physical and chemical composition of streams and lakes are largely a product of the watershed.

While agricultural activities are still responsible for degradation of the greatest expanse of impaired waters in the United States, urbanization and associated infrastructure (for example, municipal sewage) remains one of the leading causes of water quality impairment to lakes and streams in the United States (Table 8). The impacts of urbanization, or the human settlement into areas of higher population density, on aquatic systems are well documented and were recently shown to be an important factor affecting the risk of wetland conversion throughout the South (Gutzwiller and Flather 2011). Transforming a landscape from an undeveloped state to one dominated by the infrastructure associated with urban areas brings detrimental consequences to aquatic systems and the fauna inhabiting those systems. Land use changes that increase impervious surfaces (roads, rooftops, parking infrastructures, etc.) that characterize urban landscapes foster hydrologic changes impacting stream flow, sedimentation, and other physical and chemical attributes which in turn impact the makeup of the aquatic biota.

One of the defining features of urban landscapes is the construction of roads that connect areas and, in some cases, drive development into as yet undeveloped landscapes. Twenty percent of the United States' land area is directly impacted by road presence, and 50 percent is within 1,253 ft (382 m) of a road (Riitters and Wickham 2003 as cited in Wheeler and others 2005). The impact of roads on aquatic systems can be broken into three discrete phases: road construction, road presence, and urbanization (Angermeier and others 2004). The mere act of constructing roads causes physical destruction to the surrounding floodplain and watershed (Wheeler and others 2005) including removal of riparian vegetation, substantial movement of soils, and heavy equipment impacts on wetlands and other hydraulic attributes of the watershed. The greatest threat of highway construction to streams is fine sediment pollution (Wheeler and others 2005). Even with sediment control techniques, streams impacted by highway construction carried 5-12 times more fine sediments than streams not impacted (Weber and Reed 1976). Fine sediment pollution has been shown to impact macroinvertebrates and periphyton (algae and microbes attached to subsurface structures) levels and clog the gills of fish (Wheeler and others 2005) as well as alter the reproductive success of fish (Burkhead and Jelks 2001).

Roads continue to impact aquatic systems after all construction is completed and equipment has moved onto the next project. Bridge abutments and culverts may destabilize stream channels by altering stream flows, causing downstream incision of stream channels and upstream sedimentation, and serving as conduits for transporting sediment, oil, grease, and heavy metals directly to waterways. Commonly, culverts can act as impediments to fish passage to upstream or downstream habitats. Currently, the Chesapeake Bay watershed has over 5,000 miles of fish spawning habitat that remain blocked by dams, culverts, and other blockages even though 1,838 miles have been restored between 1988-2005 (www.chesapeakebay net, October 12, 2010).

Effects of Urbanization

Activities associated with urbanization are one of the leading causes of water quality impairment to lakes and streams in the United States (Table 8). Studies have demonstrated that increasing coverage of the landscape by impervious surface causes a degradation of watershed health that begins when impervious surfaces coverage exceeds 10 percent of the watershed (Arnold and Gibbons 1996, Wheeler and others 2005). The greatest changes occur in the initial stages of urbanization as compared to prolonged urbanization. Fitzpatrick and others (2005) found that base flows in streams were consistently low in watersheds with an urbanization measure of greater than 33 percent, or approximately 10 percent impervious surface. However, Cuffney and others (2010) concluded that invertebrate assemblages began to degrade quickly following disturbance of the background land cover and continued on a linear downward trend after that.

Mechanisms Resulting From Urbanization

The mechanisms that cause these impacts to the aquatic systems with greater urbanization are varied, and include changes to flow regimes and hydrography, introduction of contaminants, increases in water temperature, and increases in sedimentation. Paving 20 percent of a watershed can increase the peak discharge of the mean annual flood by an order of magnitude (Hollis 1975 as cited in Wheeler and others 2005). These increased flows can induce a variety of impacts, including increased erosion of stream banks that add fine sediments to the stream system and incision of the stream channel. Urbanization also clears riparian vegetation and reduces woody debris in aquatic systems, which is an important source of nutrient input to the stream and cover for fish and macroinvertebrates (Flebbe and Dolloff 1995). While increased peak flows are a consequence of urbanization, reduced base flows into the stream also result with increasing impervious surface in the watershed. Rather than a gradual filtering of precipitation through the soils and into aquatic systems through the base flow, impervious surfaces direct runoff immediately into waterways. Increasing impervious surface also results in higher stream water temperatures (Nelson and others 2009).

Effects on Aquatic Biota

The quantitative impact of increased urbanization has been extensively documented. Urban streams have been shown to exhibit reduced aquatic taxa richness (Garie and McIntosh 1986) and lower Index of Biotic Integrity (IBI) scores (Steedman 1988 as cited in Wheeler and others 2005). In one study, fish IBIs were low in watersheds with greater than 25 percent urban land cover; no high IBI scores were seen in watersheds with greater than 40 percent urbanization (Fitzpatrick and others 2005). One causative factor in this may have been the reduction in fish passage in urban streams. In terms of species composition, the warmer and greater instability of the physical/chemical environments in disturbed systems tends to favor more tolerant taxa. Aquatic systems in landscapes that have been fragmented and disturbed by urbanization promoted highly tolerant species but have deleterious impacts on sensitive species (Kennan and others 2005).

Although the research literature strongly points to a decline in aquatic habitat conditions with increasing urbanization, the degree to which the environment is impacted depends on a number of factors, including land use in the watershed prior to urbanization. Although fish IBIs and stream hydrology are impacted by urbanization, the extent to which streams are impacted depends on watershed characteristics such as clayey deposits, watershed slope, glacial landforms, and stormwater management practices (Fitzpatrick 2005). In a study of the effects of urbanization in nine metropolitan areas, areas that show lower effects from urbanization for invertebrates were those where urbanization progressed by the conversion of agricultural lands (row crop, pasture, and grazing lands) to urban landscapes (Cuffney and others 2010). The macroinvertebrate communities in those areas had already been impacted by agricultural activities (the top cause of water quality impairment according to the EPA) before urbanization progressed. Cuffney and others (2010: 191) concluded that "these results indicate that the efforts to mitigate effects of urbanization in areas with high levels of anteced-ent agriculture must take into account the negative effects of the agriculture when determining the levels of recovery that can be achieved." The success of popular mitigation techniques such as restoration of riparian buffers may also depend greatly on the surrounding landscape. Riparian buffers may be less able to moderate negative effects of urbanization than they do in forest or agricultural watersheds, since hydrologic alterations attributed to storm sewer and culvert installation in urban landscapes may allow water to bypass these buffers (Fitzpatrick 2005). Even in partially forested watersheds, landscape practices that promote continuous forest cover along waterways are preferable to those that result in the same extent of coverage but in a patchwork or fragmented distribution (Kennan and others 2005).

Case Study 2: Exploring Trends in Largemouth Bass Relative Abundance With MARIS _____

Nancy Nate[9] and Andrew Loftus

The Multistate Aquatic Resources Information System (MARIS) is a distributed information system designed to exchange fisheries survey information among multiple state fisheries management agencies. The design and implementation of MARIS, as well as an evaluation of its utility in assessing status and trends, was reviewed in the 2000 RPA Assessment (Loftus and Flather 2000). The USDA Forest Service has been a participant in MARIS since its inception in the mid 1990s (Beard and others 1998) and was instrumental in funding the initial foundation of this program.

In the time since the 2000 RPA Assessment, MARIS has expanded in geographic coverage and content. Data from Michigan, Wisconsin, Minnesota, Pennsylvania, New York, New Jersey, Iowa, Illinois, Wyoming, Maryland and Georgia, and limited data from Indiana and Ohio, are available in the MARIS system. Several southeastern states are evaluating their ability to contribute in 2011. At the time of the 2000 RPA Assessment, only data collected in lake and reservoir surveys were available through MARIS; now data from stream and river systems are also available. Catch-per-unit-effort data have been supplemented with population estimate data. These changes have resulted in a system that is capable of accepting data from the entire breadth of most state sampling programs.

In 2008, an assessment was conducted of the data available in MARIS at that time. This included an analysis of an assembled database from Michigan, Wisconsin, Minnesota, Pennsylvania, New York, New Jersey, and Iowa. This seven-state database contains 7,751 lake, 9,473 stream, and 489 impoundment surveys, encompassing 14,321 unique waterbodies (lakes and streams) sampled between 1944 and 2008 (Figure CS2-1).

The primary quantitative variable for lakes in MARIS is catch-per-unit-effort (CPUE), an index of fish relative abundance. Catch per unit effort data have been used to monitor stock abundance over time (for example, Hansen and others 1995), evaluate spatial distribution patterns within stocks (for example, Ward and others 2000), compare stocks across waterbodies (Nate and others 2003), and describe fish assemblages (for example, Spangler and Collins 1992). The number of sampled waterbodies with historical CPUE estimates varies greatly among the states currently participating in MARIS (Figure CS2-2), with Wisconsin, Pennsylvania, Minnesota, and New York all contributing more than 2000 estimates.

_____

[9] Dr. Nancy Nate is a research associate at the University of Wisconsin-Stevens Point.

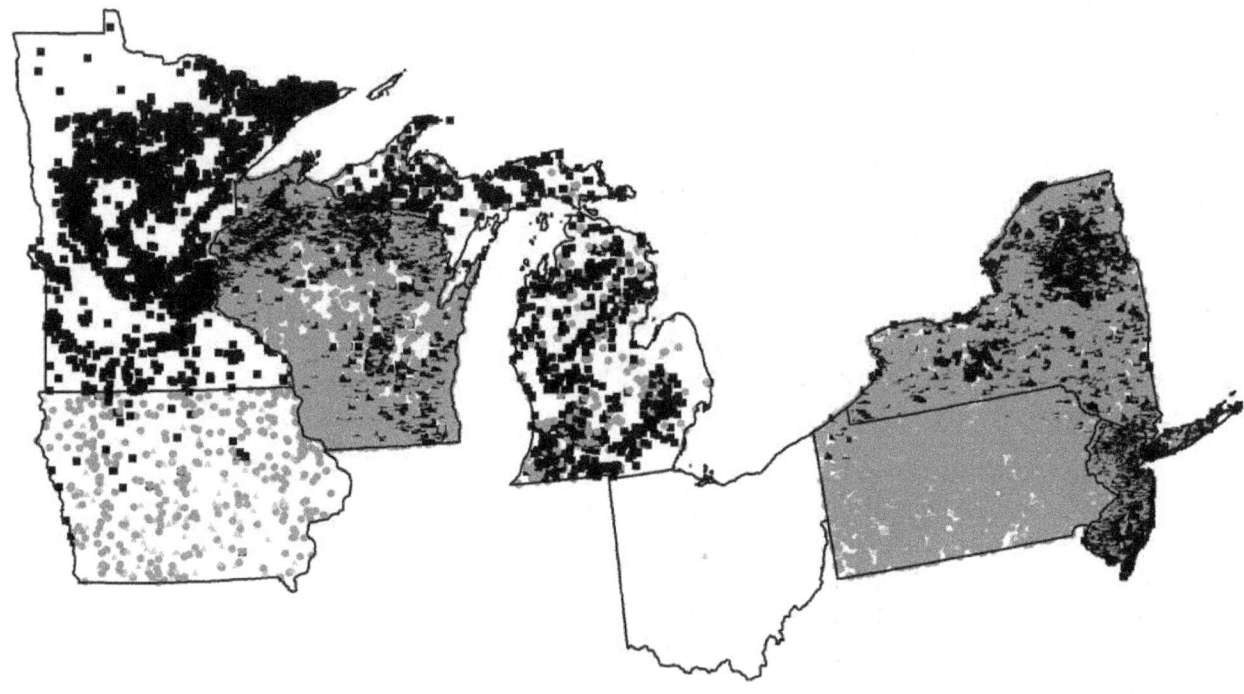

Figure CS2-1—Distribution of surveys in lakes (black squares), streams (grey circles), and impoundments (light grey triangles) by state included in the MARIS Assessment Project Database.

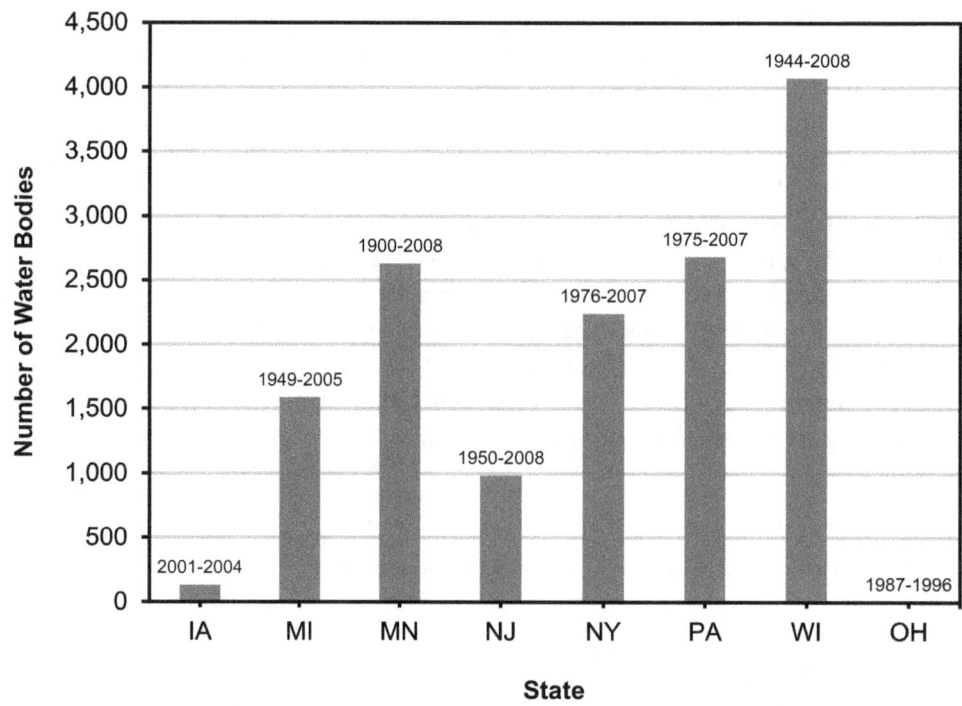

Figure CS2-2—The number of lakes, streams, and impoundments by state included in the MARIS Assessment Project Database, with the time span for CPUE data included.

Sampling methods were not necessarily standardized within states through time and were not coordinated among states represented in the MARIS dataset. However, many factors that influence catchability (how likely a particular fish species is to be captured in a specific gear) may be accounted for from variables currently stored in MARIS. Querying for specific criteria would allow post hoc standardization. For example, analyses of status and trends within single waterbodies or among many waterbodies across jurisdictional boundaries may be possible by querying for specific gear types deployed during specific season, for species that are known to be indexed well from the gear and season combination selected. The degree to which 1) actual sampling methods diverge from "standard", or 2) important aspects of standardization are not accounted for during analysis will affect the accuracy of the catch per unit effort index of relative abundance, and ultimately the conclusions about status and trends. However, in a dataset as large in scope as MARIS, any divergence from "standard" is likely to be random and not systematically occurring within or among states over time. Systematic patterns would lead to bias and inappropriate conclusions in a trend analysis. If broad general trends in species' relative abundance are revealed despite inevitable variations in methods or gear (that is, lack of true standardization), these patterns are likely to be robust and worthy of further investigation. Finally, the intended use of the data should dictate the rigor with which records are screened for inclusion in any analysis. The accuracy required for setting harvest policy on specific waters differs from accuracy required to explore regional changes in species abundance or distribution.

Example: Regional Trend in Largemouth Bass Abundance

Largemouth bass (*Micropterus salmoides*) are a species likely to be monitored by fisheries management agencies given its rank as one of the most commonly sought species by recreational anglers (see Table 13). Moreover, largemouth bass were the most prevalent species observed in lake and impoundment surveys in the MARIS assessment database— being present in 4,679 lakes and surveyed by 6 of the 7 states included in the assessment (Figure CS2-3). Of these, 1,577 lakes had three or more years of survey data available for analysis of trends on individual waterbodies.

Electro-fishing CPUE during spring when largemouth bass are spawning has been used to index largemouth bass density (McInerny and Cross 2000). Of the 4,679 lakes with largemouth bass present, 1,302 lakes had spring electro-fishing catch per hour available for regional analysis of trends in largemouth bass relative abundance (Figure CS2-4). Data from Iowa, Michigan, Minnesota, New Jersey, Pennsylvania, and Wisconsin were included in the regional analysis. Across the region, average largemouth relative abundance indexed from spring electro-fishing catch per hour increased during 1960–2008 (Figure CS2-5). Average catch per hour ranged 2–127 largemouth bass. The surface area of the lakes included in the analysis ranged 1.2-14,000 acres. The cause for the increasing trend in largemouth bass relative abundance is unknown, but stocking practices, habitat improvement, or improving climatic conditions for largemouth bass are all possible explanations that could be explored further with integration of other data types (for example, stocking records, spatially explicit land use data surrounding waterbodies, etc.). Increasing efficiency of electro-fishing gear over time could also explain an increasing trend through time, but this would have to be occurring systematically among states over time to be a plausible explanation for the pattern in Figure CS2-5.

Figure CS2-3—Lakes and impoundments with largemouth bass present in the MARIS Assessment Database. Grey circles represent lakes with 3 or more years of survey data.

Figure CS2-4—Lakes and impoundments with largemouth bass present during May electro-fishing surveys in the MARIS Assessment Database. Grey circles represent lakes with 3 or more years of survey data.

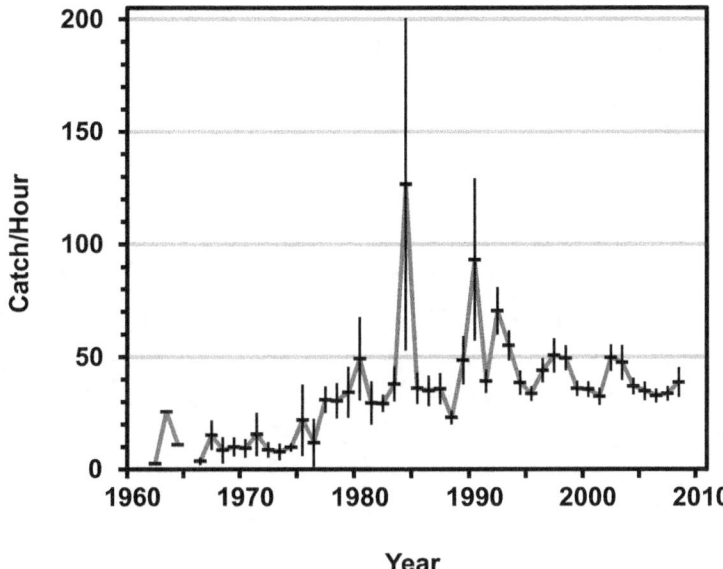

Figure CS2-5—Regional trends in largemouth bass relative abundance for spring electro-fishing surveys in the MARIS Assessment Database, 1960–2008. Catch/Hour was calculated as the yearly average ± 1 standard error for 2,780 surveys on 1,302 lakes where largemouth bass were captured during May and catch per hour (CPUE_TIME) was provided by the state.

Discussion

The process of assembling datasets by applying post-hoc standardization criteria is more likely to result in large datasets if the frequency of gear types, seasons, and metrics in the MARIS assessment database are considered. For example, electro-fishing is the most common gear type used in stream sampling, whereas electro-fishing, trap netting, and gill netting are all common gear types used in lakes and impoundments. Standardizing analyses of stream data by selecting only electro-fishing surveys will result in the largest possible dataset. As more screening criteria are applied, fewer surveys will meet all criteria and resulting datasets will decrease in size. Stream surveys most often occur during the month of July. May, September, and October are common sampling months for lakes. Not all species will be targeted during the most common sampling months, but summaries by month provide a starting point for querying MARIS data. Finally, CPUE metrics supplied by each state varied. Time-based catch per unit effort was the most common CPUE metric for stream surveys, whereas space (or distance) based CPUE was the most common metric for lakes. Various metrics of relative abundance can be combined to broaden analyses, but analyzing surveys where common metrics were supplied is more straightforward.

At present, MARIS data, which is available to anyone, can be used to examine patterns in fish distribution, species presence, trends in species relative abundance on individual waterbodies, and trends in species relative abundance by state or region across many waterbodies. The potential exists to explore shifts in fish communities over time or classify waterbodies based on morphometric characteristics that influence presence of species, or relative abundance of fishes. The robustness of these analyses depends in part on the completeness of each state's collection of these data and subsequent contribution to MARIS. The opportunities for using MARIS will increase as more historic data are included, more states become involved, more metrics are included, and with enhancements to the current structure.

Case Study 3: Status of Northwest Pacific Salmon _____

Current Situation

Salmon in the Pacific Northwest have been intensively studied since at least the latter half of the 20th century. The decline of many of these stocks has been documented in numerous publications, including in the last RPA assessment (see Loftus and Flather 2000).

Five indigenous species of salmon and one species of anadromous trout have been a dominant focus of concern in waters of the Pacific Northwest: chinook (or king) salmon (*Oncorhynchus tshawytscha*), coho (or silver) salmon (*Oncorhynchus kisutch*), sockeye salmon (*Oncorhynchus nerka*), pink (or humpback) salmon (*Oncorhynchus gorbuscha*), chum (or dog) salmon (*Oncorhynchus keta*), and steelhead trout (*Oncorhynchus mykiss*). No individual species is in danger of extinction as a whole; rather, distinct populations (also referred to as evolutionarily significant units, or ESU) are considered as threatened in some manner. Additional species such as sea run cutthroat trout are also experiencing population declines.

Factors contributing to the decline of Pacific salmon are generally related to anthropogenic induced changes to spawning and rearing habitat (Buck and Upton 2010, Loftus and Flather 2000). Excessive siltation caused by landscape changes (for example, grazing and agricultural activities that remove vegetation; urbanization; and impervious surfaces in the watershed); water removals for irrigation, consumption, and industrial uses; obstructions (for example, hydroelectric facilities, road culverts) preventing salmon from reaching spawning habitats; and direct physical changes to their spawning and rearing habitats are among the factors presenting challenges to successful reproduction of Pacific salmon (Buck and Upton 2010). Even when dams are breached or fish passage constructed to allow migrating salmon access to upstream spawning habitats, the changes to the aquatic systems behind the dams from the natural lentic system in which salmon evolved to a lotic system common to hydroelectric facilities may impact the survival of young salmon migrating back downstream. Attempts to mitigate for salmon losses and restore populations through stocking of hatchery-produced fish have had mixed success; while such stockings may enhance the number of salmon available for harvest, improper stocking techniques have resulted in the loss of genetic diversity and mixing of populations. Hatchery-produced fish generally have a lower survival than native fish, and mixed hatchery/wild stocks present a problem for harvest managers. Eighty percent of the salmon caught commercially in the Pacific northwest and northern California come from hatcheries, but allowing harvest of hatchery fish may also increase harvest of sensitive wild fish in the same system (Buck and Upton 2010).

In general, Pacific salmon have declined throughout much of their range although stocks native to Alaska tributaries are much more robust than those in the Pacific Northwest (Piccolo and others 2009, Loftus and Flather 2000). A comprehensive evaluation of all salmon, steelhead, and sea-run cutthroat trout was conducted 20 years ago by the American Fisheries Society. At that time, 214 stocks of salmon, steelhead, and sea-run cutthroat trout in the Northwest and California were at risk of extinction or of special concern and 106 were already extinct (Nehlsen and others 1991). Today, much of the focus in the Pacific Northwest is on stocks that are considered threatened, endangered, or of special concern as legally defined under the Endangered Species Act (ESA). Of the 52 distinct populations of salmon and steelhead in the Pacific Northwest, 28 (17 salmon and 11 steelhead) are currently listed under ESA (Buck and Upton 2010) (Table CS3-1).

Table CS3-1—Status, trends, and Biological Review Team (BRT) opinions of Pacific Northwest Salmon and Steelhead Populations. Base Modified from Buck and Upton 2010.

Species	Population (ESU)	Status [a]	10 Year Trend[b]	BRT opinion [c]	Federal Register citation
Coho salmon (*Oncorhynchus kisutch*)	Central California Coast	Endangered	Declining	Danger of extinction	70 FR 37160 (June 28, 2005)
	Southern Oregon/ Northern California	Threatened	Unknown	Likely to become endangered	70 FR 37160 (June 28, 2005)
	Lower Columbia River	Threatened	Stable or increasing	Danger of extinction	70 FR 37160 (June 28, 2005)
	Oregon Coast	Threatened	Stable or increasing	Likely to become endangered	73 FR 7816 (Feb. 11, 2008)
	Puget Sound/ Strait of Georgia	Species of Concern			69 FR 19975 (Apr. 15, 2004)
	Southwest Washington	Undetermined			
Chinook salmon (*Oncorhynchus tshawytscha*)	Sacramento River (winter-run)	Endangered	Stable or increasing	Danger of extinction	70 FR 37160 (June 28, 2005)
	Upper Columbia River (spring-run)	Endangered	Stable or increasing	Danger of extinction	70 FR 37160 (June 28, 2005)
	Snake River (fall-run)	Threatened	Stable or increasing	Likely to become endangered	70 FR 37160 (June 28, 2005)
	Snake River (spring-/ summer-run)	Threatened	Stable or increasing	Likely to become endangered	70 FR 37160 (June 28, 2005)
	Central Valley (spring-run)	Threatened	Stable or increasing	Likely to become endangered	70 FR 37160 (June 28, 2005)
	California coastal	Threatened	Unknown	Likely to become endangered	70 FR 37160 (June 28, 2005)
	Puget Sound	Threatened	Stable or increasing	Likely to become endangered	70 FR 37160 (June 28, 2005)
	Lower Columbia River	Threatened	Stable or increasing	Likely to become endangered	70 FR 37160 (June 28, 2005)
	Upper Willamette River	Threatened	Stable or increasing	Likely to become endangered	70 FR 37160 (June 28, 2005)
	Central Valley (fall- and late fall-run)	Species of Concern			69 FR 19975 (Apr. 15, 2004)

(continued)

Table CS3-1—(Continued).

Species	Population (ESU)	Status [a]	10 Year Trend[b]	BRT opinion [c]	Federal Register citation
Chum salmon (*Oncorhynchus keta*)	Hood Canal (summer-run)	Threatened	Stable or increasing	Likely to become endangered	70 FR 37160 (June 28, 2005)
	Columbia River	Threatened	Stable or increasing	Likely to become endangered	70 FR 37160 (June 28, 2005)
Sockeye salmon (*Oncorhynchus nerka*)	Snake River	Endangered	Unknown	Danger of extinction	70 FR 37160 (June 28, 2005)
	Ozette Lake	Threatened	Stable or increasing	Likely to become endangered	70 FR 37160 (June 28, 2005)
Steelhead trout (*Oncorhynchus mykiss*)	Southern California	Endangered	Unknown	Danger of Extinction	71 FR 834 (Jan. 5, 2006)
	Upper Columbia River	Threatened	Stable or increasing	Danger of Extinction	74 FR 42605 (Aug. 24, 2009)
	Central California Coast	Threatened	Unknown	Likely to become endangered	71 FR 834 (Jan. 5, 2006)
	South Central California Coast	Threatened	Unknown	Likely to become endangered	71 FR 834 (Jan. 5, 2006)
	Snake River Basin	Threatened	Stable or increasing	Likely to become endangered	71 FR 834 (Jan. 5, 2006)
	Lower Columbia River	Threatened	Stable or increasing	Likely to become endangered	71 FR 834 (Jan. 5, 2006)
	California Central Valley	Threatened	Unknown	Danger of Extinction	71 FR 834 (Jan. 5, 2006)
	Upper Willamette River	Threatened	Stable or increasing	Likely to become endangered	71 FR 834 (Jan. 5, 2006)
	Middle Columbia River	Threatened	Stable or increasing	Likely to become endangered	71 FR 834 (Jan. 5, 2006)
	Northern California	Threatened	Unknown	Likely to become endangered	71 FR 834 (Jan. 5, 2006)
	Puget Sound	Threatened	Declining		72 FR 26722 (May 11, 2007)
	Oregon Coast	Species of Concern			69 FR 19975 (Apr. 15, 2004)

[a] Base data: NMFS, "Snapshot of ESU Status" (http://www.nwr.noaa.gov/ESA-Salmon-Listings/upload/snapshot-7-09.pdf).
[b] NMFS 2010a
[c] Good and others (2005)

All but two of these (Puget Sound steelhead and Central California Coast coho) where 10 or more years of abundance data are available are considered "stable or increasing" (NMFS 2010a). An ESU is considered "increasing" when 75 percent or more of its populations exhibit a statistically significant upward trend in abundance. When 75 percent or more of the populations exhibit a statistically significant downward trend in abundance, it is considered as "declining." Otherwise it is classified as "stable" (NMFS 2010a).

However, trends in abundance alone may not indicate an ESU's true potential for recovery. Risk factors such as low levels of abundance, lack of access to historical spawning habitats, extirpation of subpopulations, and the lack of spatial connectivity among extant component populations are significant factors in determining recovery status (NMFS 2010a). The "viable salmonid population" concept developed by NOAA Fisheries attempts to capture some of these parameters (NMFS 2000). Likewise, Good and others (2005) developed a criterion based on self-sustainability to classify the risk level of an ESU along a gradient of: a) not likely to become endangered, b) likely to become endangered in the foreseeable future, and c) in danger of extinction. "Biological Review Teams" (BRTs) of experts used this criterion to classify the populations listed as "threatened" or "endangered" under the ESA at that time. As table CS3-1 summarizes, 8 populations were classified in the most severe category ("danger of extinction") and 19 were classified as "likely to become endangered in the foreseeable future." None were classified as "not likely to become endangered" although the BRTs were closely divided on the risk to two stocks (Middle Columbia River Steelhead and Southern Oregon/Northern California Coho) (Good and others 2005).

The Future

The future for Pacific salmon is uncertain. Although fisheries managers and researchers have vastly more knowledge than their counterparts of even 20 years ago, the forces impacting Pacific salmon are formidable. Changes to the way that society generates and utilizes electricity, produces agricultural-based food stocks, and delivers drinking water to urban consumers may necessitate wholesale changes to lifestyles. The impact of climate change [see Case Study 5: Synopsis of Climate Change Effects on Aquatic Systems] on Pacific salmon reproduction, growth, and survival, not only in their natal streams but in the open ocean, is not clearly understood (Schindler and others 2008) and poses uncertain risk to the recovery of already stressed populations. However, scientific understanding of the threats to Pacific salmon is continuing to increase and current legal protections afforded through such laws as the Endangered Species Act provide some opportunity for recovery of these stocks.

Case Study 4: Atlantic Coast Striped Bass_____

Background

Striped bass (*Morone saxatilis*) have historically been one of the most important species for both the recreational and commercial fisheries along the Atlantic coast. Commercial landings of striped bass dropped dramatically in the 1970s signaling a path toward stock collapse (see Loftus and Flather 2000), declining to a low point in the early 1980s. These populations rebounded only after dramatic fishery management efforts that significantly reduced fishing mortality on 1982 and subsequent year classes. Once considered "overfished," striped bass populations were declared fully restored in 1995 and have since been managed for a sustainable harvest (Loftus and Flather 2000). The success of striped bass restoration, largely attributable to passage of the Atlantic Striped Bass Conservation Act (P.L. 98-613), created the foundation for passage of a similar law to aid the management of other interjurisdictional Atlantic coastal species such as weakfish (*Cynoscion regalis*), summer flounder (*Paralichthys dentatus*), and others .

Historical Situation

Commercial landings of coastal Atlantic striped bass fluctuated around 4,000 metric tons (mt) in the 1960s and early 1970s before starting a precipitous downward trend in the mid 1970s (Figure CS4-1). To address this continuing decline, in 1979 Congress created the Emergency Striped Bass Study program to assist states in researching the causes behind the decline and to implement measures to arrest and reverse the decline. In 1981, the first interstate fishery management plan for striped bass was developed by the Atlantic States Marine Fisheries Commission (ASMFC) and applied to states from Maine to North Carolina. Implementation of the provisions of this plan was voluntary, with no enforcement mechanism or penalties for states that did not enact the recommended management measures. As a result, implementation was spotty most often due to political pressures within individual states, which prevented enactment of necessary restrictions on harvest.

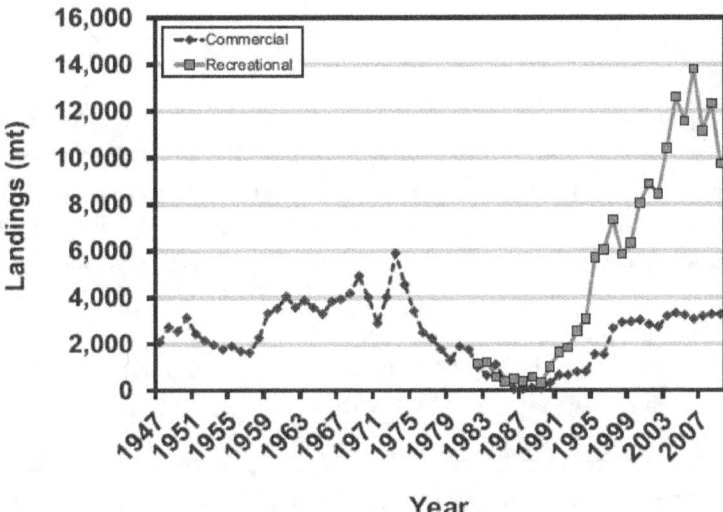

Figure CS4-1—Atlantic coast striped bass landings (source: ASMFC 2009).

Action

In 1984, the Atlantic Striped Bass Conservation Act (P.L. 98-613) was passed by Congress and signed into law by President Reagan which mandated the implementation of striped bass regulations contained within the fishery management plan developed by the ASMFC. Amendment 3 to the Striped Bass Management Plan was approved in 1985. The primary strategy contained within this amendment was to protect the 1982 year class until 95 percent of the females reached spawning age. Maryland, which had jurisdiction over the primary spawning grounds for striped bass in the Chesapeake Bay, completely closed its commercial and recreational fisheries, and other states enacted increasing size limits in their fisheries to achieve this objective. Eventually, Delaware and Virginia, other prime spawning areas, closed their fisheries in the Delaware and Chesapeake Bays respectively. Additionally, the Hudson River fishery, another prime spawning area, was closed due to PCB contamination issues.

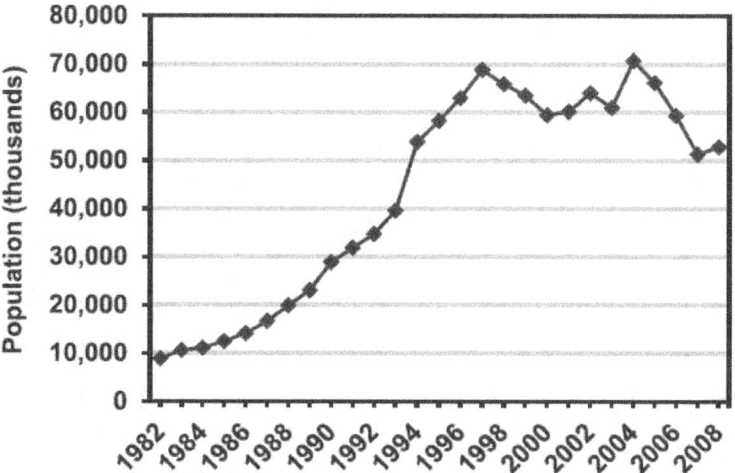

Figure CS4-2—Population of Atlantic coast striped bass (source: ASMFC 2009).

Response

A numerical trigger based on spawning success was established to signal that recovery objectives were being met and to allow relaxation of fishing restrictions. This trigger was reached in 1989. Consequently, in 1990, Amendment 4 to the interstate fishery management plan for striped bass was enacted that allowed states to reopen their fisheries at an interim fishing mortality rate that was set at ½ the estimated fishing mortality rate needed to achieve maximum sustainable yield. In 1995, coastal striped bass were declared restored by the ASMFC, and Amendment 5 was adopted to increase the target fishing mortality to 0.33, a cautionary level that was midway between the interim target (0.25) and a revised fishing mortality rate at maximum sustainable yield of 0.40 (ASMFC 2010).

By 2008, the allowable commercial harvest levels for striped bass were restored to 100 percent of the states' average landings during the 1972-1979 period, except for Delaware, which remained at the level allocated in 2002 (ASMFC 2010). In the recreational fisheries, all states continued to maintain a two fish bag limit with a minimum size limit of 28 inches, except for producer areas such as the Chesapeake Bay and Albemarle/Roanoke sound which allow fisheries with different size and bag combinations that provide "conservation equiva-lency" equal to, or more conservative than, the standard coastal fishing mortality level (ASMFC 2010). Despite this, recreational landings far exceed the commercial landings, aver-aging nearly 12,000 mt annually between 2003-2008 while the commercial landings averaged slightly more than 3,000 mt in this same time period. The federal Exclusive Economic Zone (or EEZ, generally the area from 3 miles to 200 miles offshore) remains closed to the posses-sion or harvest of striped bass.

Future

While this recovery was underway, another problem was developing that held the potential to challenge the maintenance of the record number of striped bass. Mycobacteriosis, a bacte-rial disease causing inflammation, tissue destruction, and formation of scar tissue in vital organs (spleen, kidney) of striped bass, sometimes accompanied by external lesions, was first diagnosed in the Chesapeake Bay in 1997. Up to 60 percent of striped bass in the Maryland portion of the Chesapeake Bay are infected with mycobacteriosis and in the Virginia portion mycobacteria were found in the spleens of 76 percent of striped bass collected from 1999-2001.[10] Stress factors contributing to the susceptibility of striped bass to mycobacteriosis may include dietary deficiencies resulting from depleted stocks of prey species and high summer temperatures or reduced dissolved oxygen (U.S. Geological Survey 2005).

Striped bass may be infected with this disease but have no outward sign. The actual quan-titative impact on the striped bass populations is unknown. However, according to the ASMFC (2009: 96) "…some studies have suggested that natural mortality of striped bass in Chesapeake Bay has increased since 1997 due to disease (mycobacteriosis) and reduced forage base" as well as other factors. By 2008 the total abundance of striped bass had declined 25 percent from the peak in 2004; by 2009 the legal striped bass harvest of 2.96 million fish (13,000 mt) had decreased 9 percent by number and 13 percent by weight from 2008. The recruitment (age 1 abundance) decreased from the all-time high in 2004 (22.7 million fish) to below the 12.5 million fish average for the post-recovery time period. However, the 2008 recruitment estimate of 13.3 million fish was above that average (ASMFC 2010).

In response, the ASMFC initiated an addendum to the management plan designed to reduce fishing mortality by up to 40 percent. One of the priority research needs identified by the ASMFC (2010: 15) is to "…continue analysis to determine linkages between the mycobacte-riosis outbreak in Chesapeake Bay and sex ratio of Chesapeake spawning stock, Chesapeake juvenile production, and recruitment success into coastal fisheries."

Research into the impact of mycobacteriosis as well as its causative factors is continuing. Striped bass populations are near their all-time high of the past quarter century and harvest continues to be high. However, if the trend of the latter years of this time period continue, striped bass populations and the continued relaxed levels of harvest that they support will become increasingly difficult to sustain.

---

[10] Chesapeake Bay Program, 2011. http://www.chesapeakebay net/mycobacteriosis. aspx?menuitem=19598.

Case Study 5: Synopsis of Climate Change Effects on Aquatic Systems _____

Climate change is a global phenomenon, the effects of which are playing out at local levels. Extensive research is being conducted within the global scientific community on various aspects of climate change, including its implications for aquatic systems. In the United States, climate change research is being carried out by multiple federal agencies (including the USDA Forest Service) and universities – some aimed directly at its implications to aquatic ecosystems. The purpose of this case study is not to provide a comprehensive overview of the growing literature that is focused on climate change issues associated with aquatic systems. Rather, this case study will briefly highlight some topics being addressed by researchers at the global and national scale and will review some of the potential implications of climate change on the status and trends of aquatic communities.

Global Climate Change: What Is Happening

Based largely on the 2007 report of the Intergovernmental Panel on Climate Change (IPCC), for the 100 year period 1907-2007 global atmospheric temperatures have generally increased (Solomon and others 2007). During this period, surface temperatures around the globe have increased $0.74 \pm 0.18°C$ with an even greater warming trend over the last 50 years. Eleven of the 12 years during the period 1995-2006 ranked among the warmest since surface temperature began to be collected in 1850. For the next two decades, a continued warming of approximately 0.2°C per decade is projected. This warming has been the greatest over land and at most high northern latitudes and least over Southern Ocean and parts of the North Atlantic Ocean.

Concurrent with rising temperatures, the annual average Arctic sea ice cover has shrunk since 1978 by an average of 2.7 percent per decade, with larger decreases in summer of 7.4 percent per decade. Mountain glaciers and snow cover generally have declined in both hemispheres. Snow cover is projected to continue to contract in the future.

From 1961-2003, global ocean temperatures rose by 0.10°C from the surface to 700 m depth. The oceans have become more acidic, with a 0.1 unit decrease in surface ocean pH from 1750–1994 and the rate of decrease in pH over the past 20 years has accelerated to 0.02 units per decade.

Precipitation over the last century has increased significantly across eastern parts of North America and several other regions of the world. Concurrently, extreme weather events and storm intensity have increased. The IPCC considers it very likely that precipitation increases in high latitudes and decreases in most subtropical land regions will continue the observed recent trends.

Climate Change in the United States

Climate-related changes have already been observed in the United States and its coastal waters. Changes that are particularly relevant to aquatic resources include: increases in heavy downpours, rising temperature and sea level, rapidly retreating glaciers, thawing permafrost, lengthening growing seasons, lengthening ice-free seasons in the ocean and on lakes and rivers, earlier snowmelt, and alterations in river flows (Karl and others 2009). In the United States, relative sea levels have been rising along most of the coasts at rates of 1.5–3 mm per year (Julius and West 2008). These trends are expected to continue and perhaps accelerate in some areas.

Regionally, mean annual air temperatures in the Rocky Mountains during the twentieth century increased by approximately 1 °C (Saunders and others 2008, as cited in Reiman and Isaak 2010), greater than the global average. Current projections for the western United States suggest that mean annual air temperatures will increase by another 1–3 °C by mid-century (Karl and others 2009, Reiman and Isaak 2010).

Implications for Aquatic Species Status and Trends

Aquatic communities in the United States will be affected by a combination of direct (for example, increases in water temperature) and indirect (for example, landscape changes) effects attributable to climate change. Consequently, some species may decrease in abundance and range while other species may increase in abundance and range (Isaak and others 2010). Already, there have been observed ecological changes including shifts in genetics, geographic range, ecosystem processes (for example, rates of organic matter decomposition), and the mix of life history strategies among members of the species assemblage (Reiman and Isaak 2010).

Direct Effects

Direct effects are those that result from increases in water temperature that result from increases in atmospheric temperature. Although there is less documentation of the effects of climate change in aquatic ecosystems than terrestrial (Heino and others 2009), some changes have been observed in species distributions (Hari and others 2006) and shifting prevalence of certain life history strategies (Reiman and Isaak 2010). Reiman and Isaak (2010) conclude that important changes for fishes and their habitats will be driven primarily by air temperature and precipitation. Changes to stream thermal regimes are likely to impact species distribution, abundance, growth rates, and population persistence in streams more than any other factor (Isaak and others 2010). As water temperatures increase, habitats for cold water species, such as salmon and trout, are very likely to contract. Already, Atlantic salmon are returning to the Penobscot River about two weeks ahead of when they migrated historically. This acceler-ated spawning schedule causes the young fish to utilize their internal yolk sac too early in the spring and are released into the rivers to feed before the water is warm enough to support the invertebrates they need for survival (http://www.fws.gov/northeast/climatechange/stories/salmon.html). Isaak and others (2010) concluded that the impacts of a warming climate have begun to alter temperatures and thermal habitat distributions in streams across the Boise River basin. The impacts of these changes vary with species; these changes are not expected to alter the status of rainbow trout in this basin due to the extent of the habitats that they are able to occupy, but 8-16 percent of the habitat suitable for bull trout in this basin could become unsuitable each decade due to rising water temperatures, thus making bull trout one of the more vulnerable salmonids to climate-induced population declines and range shifts.

Indirect Effects

Indirect effects result from the impacts of climate change on aspects external to the aquatic ecosystem. Changing watershed landscapes, such as altered forest and riparian communi-ties, change the amount and character of inputs such as sediment entering aquatic systems.

This, combined with wildfire activity, will change inputs of sediment and large wood, and these basic channel constituents will be routed differently by hydrologic regimes that are also evolving (Barnett and others 2008; Miller and others 2003, as cited in Reiman and Isaak 2010). Predicting the expected impacts on aquatic resources from indirect effects is particularly difficult and highly uncertain.

Combined Effects

Nelson and others (2009) investigated combined effects of climate change and urbanization discussed in a related case study [see Case Study 1: Impacts of Urbanization on Fisheries and Aquatic Ecosystems]. Overall, they found that the effects of existing stressors on aquatic systems (for example, urbanization) and climate change will threaten the viability of existing fish community structure in the piedmont streams that they analyzed. Although both factors produced detrimental effects to the systems, climate change effects were the most dominant, due in large part to increases in precipitation and resulting changes in runoff and hydrologic features of the streams. Their results suggested that 50–75 percent of the fish species in these streams would be highly stressed under all future climate scenarios. Moreover, declines in abundance are likely for many species, including species that comprise the important cold-water (trout) and warmwater (bass, sunfish) recreational fisheries. Wenger and others (2011) project that a combination of water temperature changes and shifts in hydrologic events will result in an average decline in habitat for trout species of 47 percent in the interior western United States. Specifically, their modeling analysis projects that cutthroat trout will lose 58 percent of existing habitat, brook trout and brown trout will lose 77 percent and 48 percent, respectively, and rainbow trout, 35 percent based on current conditions and assuming that current trends continue.

Most aquatic systems in the United States are already under multiple stresses. Coastal and near-shore ecosystems are impacted by urbanization as Americans have migrated to the coasts, rising sea level threatens low lying areas, and increasing acidification of ocean waters is altering near-shore marine habitats. A distinct decline in horseshoe crab numbers has occurred that parallels climate change associated with the end of the last Ice Age (Faurby and others 2010) – a trend that is expected to continue in the future given predicted climate change. In streams throughout the western United States, growing human populations and water supply needs combined with impacts of climate change (for example, warmer atmospheric temperatures, increased precipitation, and greater wildfire incidence) will combine to threaten the integrity of existing aquatic systems (Karl and others 2009, Isaak and others 2010). The extent to which aquatic systems will be affected will depend on unique features of each aquatic system and watershed, the magnitude of realized climate change, the degree of ecosystem sensitivity, and the availability of adaptation options for effective management responses (Julius and West 2008). Some of the ecosystem services currently provided by aquatic systems will be threatened by climate change, while others will be enhanced (Karl and others 2009).

Conclusion

Climate change will lead to some irreversible impacts on aquatic systems. Some of these impacts will be as drastic as extirpation of currently vulnerable species, dramatic range shifts for other species, and wholesale shifts in aquatic community structure. Some more tolerant species may sustain their populations or even thrive in these changing conditions (Nelson and others 2009). Changes in the climate system will continue into the future regardless of any potential emissions mitigation (Julius and West 2008). So, what can resource managers do about it? Reiman and Isaak (2010) suggest six main management actions:

- Enhance resistance and resilience, such as reducing non-climate stresses, conserving critical habitat re-connecting streams and habitats, and conserving genetic and pheno-typic diversity.
- Prioritize limited resources by considering the relative vulnerability of specific popula-tions and likelihood of success of potential actions.
- Facilitate transitions to new conditions.
- Develop local information.
- Coordinate efforts.

Many existing best management practices for "traditional" stressors of concern may be applied to mitigate stressors resulting from climate change (Julius and West 2008). These authors recommend similar measures as Reiman and Isaak (2010) including protecting key ecosystem features, reducing anthropogenic stresses, protecting variant forms of a species or ecosystem so that, regardless of the climatic changes that occur, there will be areas that survive, maintaining more than one ecosystem or population, and establishing refugia that are less affected by climate change to protect vulnerable species.

Table CS5-1—Observed trends and issues for the future resulting from climate change in the United States (Karl and others 2009)

Region	Observed trends	Key issues for the future
Northwest	o Annual average temperature rose 1.5°F over the past century, with some areas experiencing increases up to 4°F. o The region's average temperature is projected to rise another 3 to 10°F in this century. o Increases in winter precipitation and decreases in summer precipitation are projected. o Impacts related to changes in snowpack, streamflows, sea level, forests, and other aspects are already underway.	• Declining springtime snowpack leads to reduced summer streamflows. • Increase in insect outbreaks, wildfires, and changing species composition in forests. • Salmon and other coldwater species will experience stresses from rising water temperatures and declining summer streamflows. • Sea-level rise along coastlines will result in increased erosion and the loss of land.
Southwest	o Recent warming has been among the most rapid in the nation. o Declines in spring snowpack and Colorado River flow. o Projected continued strong warming. o Projected summertime temperature increases are greater than the annual average increases in parts of the region. o Water cycle changes are projected, which signal a serious water supply challenge. o The prospect of future droughts becoming more severe due to warming is a significant concern.	• Water supplies become increasingly scarce. • Increasing temperature, drought, wildfire, and invasive species will accelerate transformation of the landscape. • Increased frequency and altered timing of flooding will increase risks to people, ecosystems, and infrastructure. • Unique tourism and recreation opportunities are likely to suffer. • Cities and agriculture face increasing risks from a changing climate.

(Continued)

Table CS5-1—(Continued)

Region	Observed trends	Key issues for the future
Great Plains	o Average temperatures have risen throughout the Great Plains, with the largest increases occurring in the winter months and over the northern states. o Relatively cold days are becoming less frequent and relatively hot days more frequent. o Temperatures are projected to continue to increase. o Summer increases are projected to be larger than those in winter in the southern and central Great Plains. o Conditions are expected to become wetter in the north and drier in the south. o Projected changes include more frequent extreme events such as heat waves, droughts, and heavy rainfall.	o Projected increases in temperature, evaporation, and drought frequency. Agriculture, ranching, and natural lands, already under pressure due to an increasingly limited water supply, are stressed by rising temperatures. o Climate change is affecting native plant and animal species by altering key aquatic habitats. o Shifts in the region's population from rural areas to urban centers will interact with a changing climate, resulting in a variety of consequences.
Midwest/ Great Lakes	o Average temperatures have risen in recent decades, with the largest increases in winter. o The length of the frost-free or growing season has been extended by one week. o Heavy downpours are twice as frequent as they were a century ago. o Both summer and winter precipitation have been above average for the last three decades, the wettest period in a century. o A decrease in lake ice, including on the Great Lakes. o Since the 1980s, large heat waves have become more frequent than any time in the last century, other than the 1930s. o The observed patterns of temperature increases and precipitation changes are projected to continue.	o Increasing heat waves, reduced air quality, and increasing insect and waterborne diseases during the summer. o Increase in precipitation in winter and spring, more heavy downpours, and greater evaporation in summer would lead to more periods of both floods and water deficits. o Increases in heat waves, floods, droughts, insects, and weeds will present increasing challenges to managing crops, livestock, and forests. o Native species are very likely to face increasing threats from rapidly changing climate conditions, pests, diseases, and invasive species moving in from warmer regions.
Southeast	o Annual average temperature has risen 2°F since 1970, with the greatest seasonal increase in the winter months. o A 30 percent increase in fall precipitation over most of the region but a decrease in fall precipitation in South Florida. o Summer precipitation has decreased over almost the entire region. The percentage of the Southeast in moderate to severe drought increased over the past three decades. o There has been an increase in heavy downpours. o The power of Atlantic hurricanes has increased since 1970, associated with an increase in sea surface temperature. o The number of very hot days is projected to rise at a faster rate than average temperatures. o Average annual temperatures are projected to rise 4.5°F to 9°F with a 10.5°F increase in summer. o Sea-level rise is projected to accelerate, increasing coastal inundation and shoreline retreat. The intensity of hurricanes is likely to increase.	o Increases in air and water temperatures will cause heat-related stresses for people, plants, and animals. o Decreased water availability is very likely to affect the region's economy as well as its natural systems. o Sea-level rise and the likely increase in hurricane intensity and associated storm surge will be among the most serious consequences of climate change. o Ecological thresholds are likely to be crossed throughout the region, causing major disruptions to ecosystems and to the benefits they provide to people. o Quality of life will be affected by increasing heat stress, water scarcity, severe weather events, and reduced availability of insurance for at-risk properties.

(Continued)

Table CS5-1—(Continued)

Region	Observed trends	Key issues for the future
Northeast	o Annual average temperature has increased by 2°F since 1970, with winter temperatures rising twice this much with more frequent very hot days. o A longer growing season. o Increase in heavy downpours, less winter precipitation falling as snow and more as rain. o Reduced snowpack, earlier break-up of winter ice on lakes and rivers, earlier spring snowmelt resulting in earlier peak river flows, rising sea surface temperatures, and rising sea level.	o Increasing problems for human health, especially in urban areas. o Agricultural production, including dairy, fruit, and maple syrup, is likely to be adversely affected as favorable climates shift. o Severe flooding due to sea-level rise and heavy downpours is likely to be more frequent. o Adverse impacts on winter recreation and the industries that rely upon it. o The center of lobster fisheries is projected to continue its northward shift and the cod fishery on Georges Bank is likely to be diminished.
Alaska	o Over the past 50 years, annual average temperature has increased 3.4°F, while winters have warmed by 6.3°F, warming at more than twice the rate of the rest of the United States. o Earlier spring snowmelt, reduced sea ice, widespread glacier retreat, and permafrost warming. o Projected increases in precipitation with simultaneous increases in evaporation due to higher air temperatures, will lead to drier conditions overall, with reduced soil moisture. Average annual temperatures are projected to rise between 5 and 13°F by late this century.	o Longer summers and higher temperatures are causing drier conditions. o Insect outbreaks and wildfires are increasing. o Lakes are declining in area. o Thawing permafrost damages roads, runways, water and sewer systems, and other infrastructure. o Coastal storms increase risks to villages and fishing fleets. o Displacement of marine species will affect key fisheries.
Hawaii and U.S. Affiliated Islands	o Small islands are vulnerable to sea-level rise, coastal erosion, extreme weather events, coral reef bleaching, ocean acidification, and contamination of freshwater resources with saltwater. o The islands have experienced rising temperatures and sea level in recent decades. o Projections for the rest of this century suggest continued increases in air and ocean surface temperatures in both the Pacific and Caribbean. o An overall decrease in rainfall in the Caribbean, an increased frequency of heavy downpours nearly everywhere, and increased rainfall during the summer months (rather than the normal rainy season in the winter months) for the Pacific. o Hurricane wind speeds and rainfall rates are likely to increase. o Island coasts will be at increased risk of inundation.	o Availability of freshwater is likely to be reduced. o Island communities, infrastructure, and ecosystems are vulnerable to coastal inundation due to sea-level rise and coastal storms. o Climate changes affecting coastal and marine ecosystems will have major implications for tourism and fisheries.

Case Study 6: National Fish Habitat Assessment[11] _____

Introduction

The National Fish Habitat Action Plan (NFHAP, www.fishhabitat.org) was formally adopted by the states (represented by the Association of Fish and Wildlife Agencies), the U.S. Department of the Interior, and the U.S. Department of Commerce in early 2006. The USDA Forest Service participates in NFHAP through leadership positions on the National Fish Habitat Board, national office staff participation in the Federal Agency Caucus, and Forest Service staff participation on various working groups and national fish habitat partnerships.

The focus of the NFHAP "…is to protect, restore and enhance the nation's fish and aquatic communities through partnerships that foster fish habitat conservation and improve the quality of life for the American people."[12] This mission will be fulfilled through the following actions:

- Protect and maintain intact and healthy aquatic systems.
- Prevent further degradation of fish habitats that have been adversely affected.
- Reverse declines in the quality and quantity of aquatic habitats to improve the overall health of fish and other aquatic organisms.
- Increase the quality and quantity of fish habitats that support a broad natural diversity of fish and other aquatic species.

An initial task of the NFHAP was the development of the first-ever condition analysis of all fish habitats within the United States. This assessment has relied on existing national level (and in some cases large regional level) datasets of known stressors to aquatic habitats.

Jelks and others (2008) reported that the number of freshwater fish taxa considered to be "imperiled" or extinct in the United States increased 179 percent between 1979 and 2008 and nearly doubled in the last 10 years of that period. Human activities were listed as a contributing factor in the majority of these instances. The purpose of the NFHAP assessment approach was intended to clarify the potential specific causes on a nationwide scale so that national level planning could be more effective and individual partnerships could potentially target the most deleterious agents in their watershed for restoring fish habitats.

Methodology

The inland NFHAP assessment focused on streams and rivers of the coterminous United States using the 1:100,000 level National Hydrography Dataset Plus (NHDPlus) as the spatial framework. To predict the condition of fish habitats, landscape disturbance was analyzed for every river through a consistent process. This process assumed that landscape scale patterns and human activities for the variables measured correspond to patterns in local scale stressors.

---

[11] Based on: National Fish Habitat Board, 2010 and Wang and others 2011.
[12] National Fish Habitat Action Plan 2006 available at: http://www.fishhabitat.org/documents/plan/
National_Fish_Habitat_Action_Plan.pdf

Datasets representing natural characteristics (catchment elevation and slope, mean annual air temperature and precipitation, catchment area, soil permeability rates) and disturbance factors that were: (1) meaningful for assessing fish habitat; (2) consistent across the entire study area in the way that they were assembled; and (3) representative of conditions in the past 10 years were applied to the development of the assessment. Anthropogenic variables were derived from 17 datasets representing urban land use, human population density, road density, grazing and pasture use, percent row crop agriculture, farm fertilizer applications, ground and surface water usage, National Pollution Discharge Elimination Sites, Toxic Release Inventory sites, National Superfund sites, and mine density. For rivers in the coterminous United States, these variables were collectively analyzed in the categories of:

- Urban/Human settlement (percent urban land use; human population density; road density)
- Livestock and grazing (percent pasture and hay in the watershed)
- Agriculture (percent row crop agriculture in the watershed)
- Point source pollution data (numbers of National Pollution Discharge Elimination Sites, Toxic Release Inventory sites, and National Superfund sites)
- Habitat fragmentation (numbers of dams and road crossings), and
- Mine density.

Streams were scored according to their condition as indicated by these variables in each location.

Although limited data on fish presence were available, data from national sampling programs (EPA's Environmental Monitoring and Assessment Program, Regional Environmental Monitoring and Assessment Program, and NAWQA) and contributed by state agencies were used to calibrate the habitat condition scores on an ecologically defined regional basis. Where fish data were available, they were analyzed with human disturbance variables to identify the response of a set of indicator fish species to the different disturbance variables in each region. The resulting condition estimates that corresponded to the sensitivity of regionally specific fish groups were then used to determine the final habitat condition score. Stream segments in good condition were expected to have a low risk of habitat degradation and streams in poor condition a high risk of habitat degradation.

In Alaska and Hawaii, a variation of the methodology was used due to the limited data available in these states. Principal component analysis was employed among the various categories of variables to arrive at a single habitat score that indicated the condition of the stream.

For estuaries, habitat stress was measured by river discharge, pollutant levels, eutrophication, and urban, agricultural, and estuarine wetland land cover. A single disturbance score was calculated for each estuary based on measures of river discharge, pollution, land cover, land cover change, and eutrophication.

Results[13]

Nationwide

In the coterminous United States, 27 percent of the stream miles are at high or very high risk of current habitat degradation and 44 percent are at low or very low risk (Figure CS6-1). As with water quality assessments highlighted elsewhere in this report, urban development, livestock grazing, agriculture, and point source pollution had higher risk of degradation, as did areas with high numbers of mines and dams. Rural areas without these disturbance factors (for example, Northeast, Southwest, and Pacific Coast States; see Figure CS6-2 for regional definitions) were at lower risk of degradation based on the variables analyzed. The estuaries showed a pattern that is consistent with increased human population growth in coastal areas—namely that the percent of estuarine area considered at high or very high risk of habitat degradation was much greater (53 percent) than inland land areas. Twenty-three percent of estuarine area is at low or very low risk.

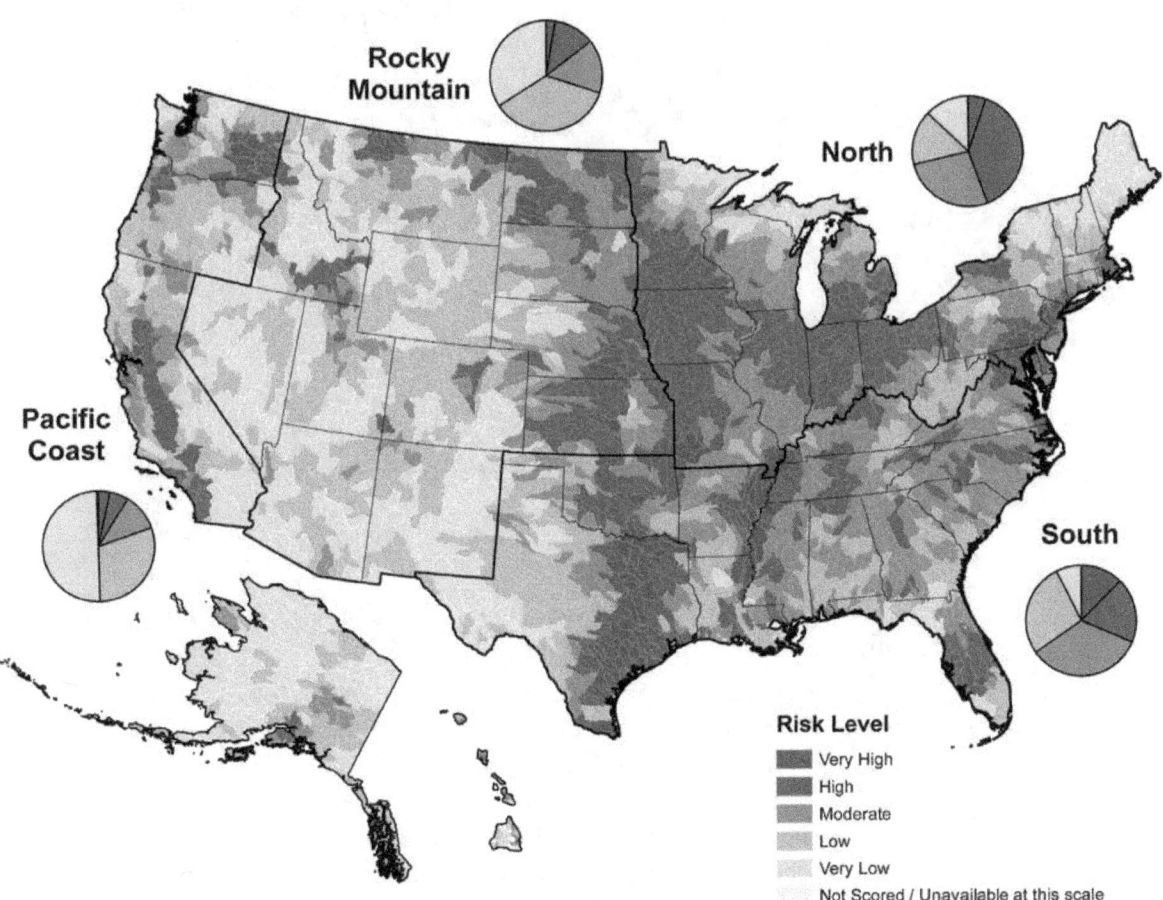

Figure CS6-1—Relative condition of riverine and near coastal habitat based on the variables analyzed (National Fish Habitat Board 2010).

---

[13] Map-based results can be viewed at http://ecosystems.usgs.gov/fishhabitat/

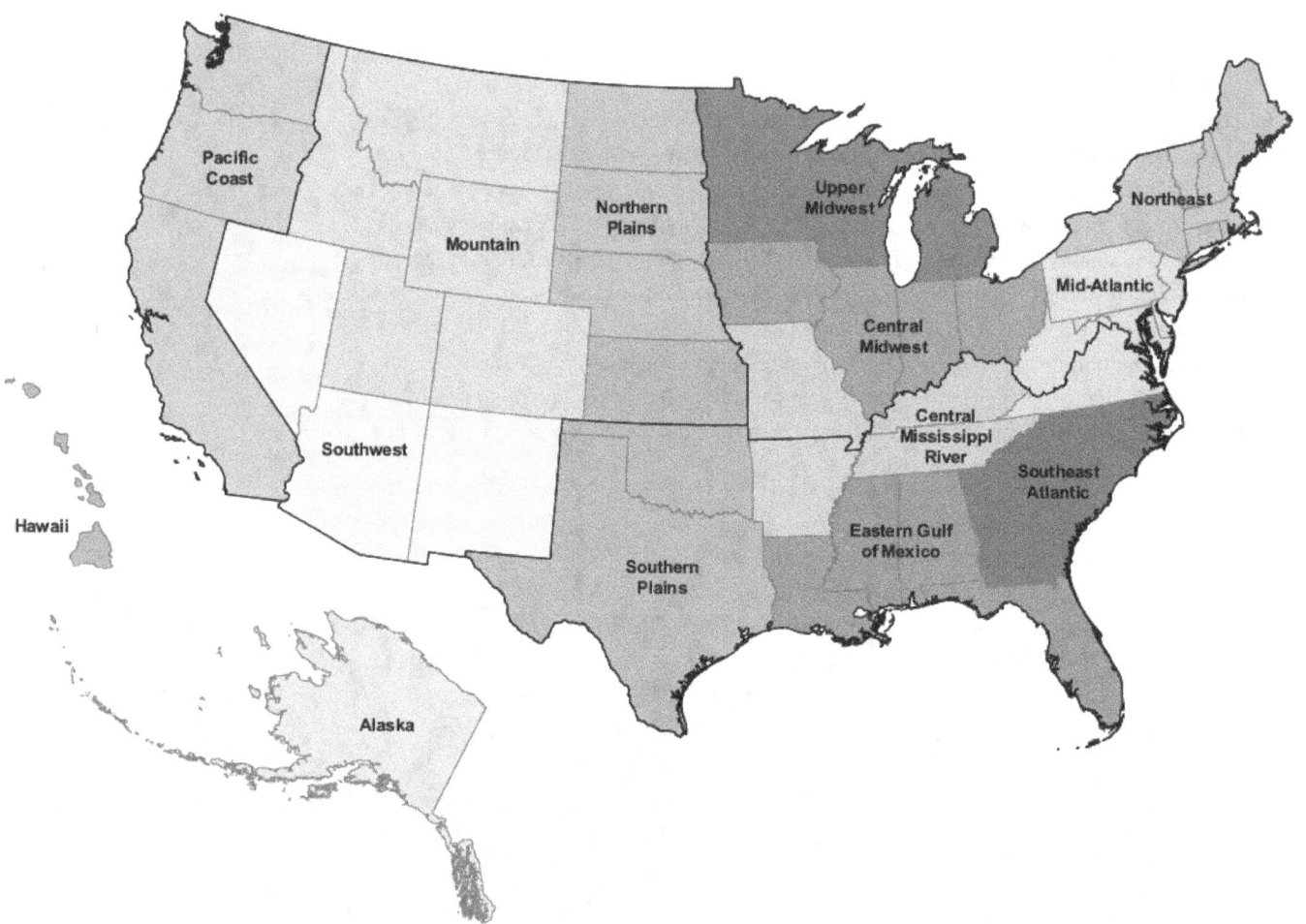

Figure CS6-2—Regional partitions used in the National Fish Habitat Assessment (National Fish Habitat Board 2010).

Northeast States (New York, Connecticut, Rhode Island, Massachusetts, Vermont, Maine, New Hampshire)

Nearly 60 percent of the stream miles in the northeastern states have a low or very low risk of habitat degradation and 16 percent have high or very high risk; 44 percent of the estuarine area is at high or very high risk. Stream conditions in the northern parts of Maine and New Hampshire and the Adirondack Mountain region of in New York is at very low risk of degradation from the factors assessed. The habitats at highest risk of degradation occur in the farmlands of northeast New York where row crops and pasture are dominant influences, along the Hudson and Connecticut rivers where urbanization and farming occur, and in urban areas of the region. Estuarine areas have the lowest risk of degradation along Maine's coast and the highest risk of degradation in Long Island Sound, Massachusetts Bay, and Narragansett Bay, where excess nutrients and sources of pollution in the watershed are a key issue.

Mid-Atlantic States (Pennsylvania, New Jersey, Delaware, Maryland, Virginia, West Virginia)

Thirty-three percent of the stream miles in this region are at low or very low risk of degradation with 29 percent at high or very high risk. Stream habitat in most of West Virginia is at low risk of degradation from the factors assessed, but it should be noted that legacy mining and barrier issues have not yet been fully assessed. Areas with the highest risk of degradation include northeast New Jersey, southeast and southwest Pennsylvania, central Maryland, and northern Virginia. Row crops, pasture, and urbanization all affect habitats in these areas. Chesapeake Bay shows a very high risk of habitat degradation due to excess nutrients and a highly altered watershed, while Delaware Bay and other estuaries in the region also show a high risk of degradation due to watersheds that are highly altered. Ninety-five percent of the estuarine area in the mid-Atlantic states is at high or very high risk of current habitat degradation.

Southeast Atlantic States (Georgia, South Carolina, North Carolina)

The greatest proportion (44 percent) of the stream miles in this region are at moderate risk of habitat degradation with 33 percent at low or very low risk. With one of the highest population growth rates in the country, this region contains areas of fish habitat at very high risk of degradation due to urbanization around the large metropolitan growth areas of Charlotte, Raleigh/Durham, and Atlanta. Areas with a low risk of degradation include the mountains of western North Carolina and parts of the coastal plain of all three states. Eighty-two percent of the estuarine area is at high or very high risk of degradations, influenced by the relatively large Albemarle-Pamlico Sound, which has a high risk of impairment due to agricultural runoff. Many of the smaller estuaries are generally at low risk of degradation.

Upper Midwest States (Minnesota, Wisconsin, Michigan)

Forty-two percent of the river miles in this region are at moderate risk of habitat degradation, with 29 percent at high or very high risk. Fish habitat in the northern parts of Michigan, Wisconsin, and Minnesota are at low or very low risk of degradation from the factors assessed. Areas that are at very high risk of degradation occur near large metropolitan areas of Minneapolis, Detroit, and Chicago. Streams in southwest Minnesota reported to have a high risk of degradation generally due to the effects of row crop agriculture and urbanization.

Central Midwest States (Ohio, Indiana, Illinois, Iowa)

Forty-six percent of the stream miles in this region are at high or very high risk of habitat degradation with 47 percent being at moderate risk. A large proportion of aquatic habitat in Iowa has a high risk of degradation from the factors assessed, mainly row crop agriculture. Illinois, north central Indiana, and northeastern Ohio also contain areas where habitat has a high risk of degradation from agriculture or a very high risk of degradation from urbanization.

Central Mississippi River States (Missouri, Arkansas, Kentucky, Tennessee)

Forty percent of the stream miles in this region have a very high predicted risk of degradation and 34 percent have moderate risk from the factors assessed, mainly due to row crop agriculture. Areas with a high risk of degradation also occur in southwest Missouri and central Kentucky and Tennessee, where pasture is the main source of habitat degradation. Areas with low risk of habitat degradation occur in the mountains of eastern Kentucky and western Arkansas.

Eastern Gulf of Mexico States (Florida, Alabama, Mississippi, Louisiana)

Thirty-two percent of the stream miles in this region have a high or very high risk of degradation from the factors assessed; 41 percent are rated as low or very low risk. Much of central Florida is at very high risk of habitat degradation due to use of the area as pasture, as is a large area in southwestern Louisiana where row crops and pasture both contribute to habitat degradation. Large areas along the Mississippi River and in highly urbanized southeastern Florida are at very high risk of degradation. The panhandle of Florida contains areas of habitat with a low risk of degradation. The estuaries along most of the eastern Gulf of Mexico have a moderate (53 percent) to low risk of degradation with the exception of Tampa Bay and Pine Island Sound, where urbanization and pollution in the watershed negatively affect the estuary.

Southern Plains States (Texas, Oklahoma, Kansas)

Thirty-eight percent of the stream miles in this region are at high or very high risk of degradation, while 31 percent are at low or very low risk. Urbanization in eastern Texas and row crops and pasture in western Kansas are responsible for areas with a very high risk of degradation due to the factors assessed. Habitat with a very low risk of degradation occurs in central Texas and eastern Kansas. Sixty-five percent of the estuarine area of Texas is at high or very high risk of degradation due to highly altered watersheds.

Northern Plains States (North Dakota, South Dakota, Nebraska)

Thirty-five percent of the stream miles in this region are at a very high risk of degradation from the factors assessed, with heavy concentrations of aquatic habitat in southwest North Dakota, central and southeastern South Dakota, and southern Nebraska being impacted by row crops, pasture, and road crossings. Conversely, large tracts with low risk occur in north central Nebraska and western South Dakota where these factors are not as intense.

Mountain States (Colorado, Idaho, Montana, Utah, Wyoming)

Sixty-four percent of the stream miles in this region are at low or very low risk of degradation with only 17 percent at high or very high levels. The habitats with the highest risk of degradation occur in all five states, related to row crops in southeast Idaho, pasture in northern Montana, and urbanization in a areas around Denver and Salt Lake City. Areas with a very low risk of degradation occur in central Idaho, parts of northwest Montana, and northwest Wyoming, particularly where large tracts of parks, wilderness areas, and other protected lands occur.

Southwest States (Arizona, New Mexico, Nevada)

Seventy-six percent of the stream miles in this region were assessed to have low or very low risk of disturbance (note that water diversions and drought, common problems in this area, were not considered in this analysis). Areas of fish habitat with a very high risk of degradation (9 percent of stream miles region wide) occur in southwest Arizona where urbanization, dams, and road crossings are of greatest concern. Northwest Arizona, southern Utah, and other parts of these states contain areas with a very low risk of aquatic habitat degradation.

Pacific Coast States (California, Oregon, Washington)

Fifty-eight percent of the stream miles in this region are at low or very low risk of disturbance. Overall, 25 percent of the region is at high or very high risk of disturbance, with California's Central Valley, a portion of northeastern Oregon, and eastern Washington bearing much of this, principally due to row crops. The western urbanized areas from the Canadian border south to Eugene, Oregon, are also at high risk of degradation as well as the Los Angeles and San Diego areas. Areas with a low risk of degradation occur in northern Washington, central Oregon, and eastern California. With the exception of Puget Sound, estuaries in Washington, Oregon, and northern California have a low risk of degradation, whereas the estuaries of central and southern California are generally at high risk of degradation from altered flows and watersheds that are highly altered with a high number of pollution sources. Fifty-three percent of the estuarine area in the region has a low or very low risk of disturbance for the factors considered with 42 percent being at high or very high risk.

Alaska

As indicated earlier, the assessment factors used for Alaska differed from the coterminous United States and therefore cannot be directly compared. However, most of Alaskan fish habitat is relatively undeveloped, and the state has some of the least disturbed aquatic habitat in the country. However, localized areas at risk for habitat degradation exist around metropolitan areas due to the effects of roads and urbanization.

Hawaii

As with Alaska, the assessment factors used for Hawaii differed from the coterminous United States and therefore cannot be directly compared. Inland aquatic systems in Hawaii have been extensively developed for drinking water and agricultural irrigation. A very cursory analysis for those rivers that flow to the ocean was conducted but cannot be compared to the coterminous United States. Areas of urbanization on the islands of Hawaii, Oahu, and Maui are most at risk for habitat degradation from the factors assessed. Areas with a low risk of degradation occur in higher elevations away from the coast or away from the main urbanized areas.

Use of the Information

The habitat conditions outlined in this report reflect the limited range of variables analyzed that represent or are correlated with particular habitat stressors. Some factors very important in specific geographic regions may not be included. Factors known to affect the condition of aquatic habitats that lacked spatially extensive and consistent collection methods were not included in the condition index. For example, although large dams and road crossings (that are in the analysis) could be used as surrogate indicators for fish passage obstructions, actual smaller scale obstructions (for example, culverts or conversely fishways around dams) are not reflected in the analysis nor hydrologic metrics (flow, connectivity, etc.). Neither are some of the significant factors leading to species endangerment such as invasive species (Jelks and others 2008). However, because large scale stressors to aquatic systems such as urbanization, agriculture, and road building are represented in the analysis, it has utility for evaluating major threats to aquatic systems at the geographic scale (1:100K) analyzed.

While the national level compilation of scores at broader spatial units is useful for policy makers and planners in assessing national budgetary and program needs, the finer scale watershed analyses will be most useful to on-the-ground efforts to protect, restore, and enhance habitats for healthy fish populations. These analyses represent the initial attempt to characterize habitat factors impacting fish populations and will be refined as additional national scale data become available. The data download and mapping capability are made available to Fish Habitat Partnerships and others through an interactive web tool that will enable these partnerships to visualize specific habitat factors influencing the local and catchment watersheds (http://ecosystems.usgs.gov/fishhabitat). It is anticipated that this delivery mechanism will facilitate application of the assessment to the implementation of restoration projects and likely result in an information exchange that will help to refine data elements for use in future assessments.

References

Allan, J.D.; Erickson, D.L.; Fay, J. 1997. The influence of catchment land use on stream integrity across multiple spatial scales. Freshwater Biology 37: 149-161.

American Sportfishing Association. 2007. State and national economic effects of fishing, hunting and wildlife-related recreation on U.S. Forest Service-Managed Lands. (04-PA-11132422-315). Washington, DC: U.S. Department of Agriculture, Forest Service. 63 p.

Atlantic States Marine Fisheries Commission (ASMFC). 2009. 2009 stock assessment report for Atlantic striped bass. Washington, DC: Atlantic Striped Bass Technical Committee. 281 p.

Atlantic States Marine Fisheries Commission (ASMFC). 2010. 2010 review of the Atlantic States marine Fisheries Commission fishery management plan for Atlantic striped bass (Morone saxatilis) 2009 fishing year. Washington, DC. 35 p.

Angermeier, P.L.; Wheeler, A.P.; Rosenberger, A.E. 2004. A conceptual framework for assessing impacts of roads on aquatic biota. Fisheries 29(12): 19-29.

Arnold, C.L.; Gibbons, C.J. 1996. Impervious surface coverage: the emergence of a key environmental indicator. Journal of the American Planning Association 62: 243-258.

Barnett, T. P.; Pierce, D. W.; Hidalgo, H. G.; [and others]. 2008. Human induced changes in the hydrology of the western United States. Science 319: 1080-1083.

Bonar, S.A.; Hubert, W.A.; Willis D.W., (eds.). 2009. Standard methods for sampling North American freshwater fishes. Bethesda, MD: American Fisheries Society. 335 p.

Beard, T.D., Jr.; Austen, D.; Brady, S.J.; [and others]. 1998. The multi-state aquatic resources information system: an internet system to access fisheries information in the upper midwestern United States. Fisheries 23(5): 14-18.

Branch, T.A.; Jensen, O.P; Ricard, D.; [and others]. 2011. Contrasting global trends in marine fishery status obtained from catches and from stock assessments. Conservation Biology 25: 777-786

Buck, E.H.; Upton, H.F. 2010. Pacific salmon and steelhead trout: managing under the Endangered Species Act. Congressional Research Service Report for Congress 98-666. 10 p.

Burkhead, N.M.; Jelks, H.L. 2001. Effects of suspended sediment on the reproductive success of the tricolor shiner, a crevice spawning minnow. Transactions of the American Fisheries Society 130: 959-968.

Cuffney, T.F.; Brightbill, R.A.; May, J.T.; Waite, I.R. 2010. Responses of benthic macro-invertebrates to environmental changes associated with urbanization in nine metropolitan areas. Ecological Applications 20: 1384-1401.

Daily, G.C. 1997. Introduction: What are ecosystem services? In: Daily, G.C., ed. Natures services: societal dependence on natural ecosystems. Washington, DC: Island Press: 1–10.

Deacon, J.E.; Kobetich, G.; Williams, J.D.; Contreras, S. 1979. Fishes of North America endangered, threatened, or of special concern: 1979. Fisheries 4(2): 29-44.

Faurby, S.; King, T.L.; Obst, M.; [and others]. 2010. Population dynamics of American horseshoe crabs—historic climatic events and recent anthropogenic pressures. Molecular Ecology 19: 3088-3100.

Fausch, K.D.; Torgersen, C.E.; Baxter, C.V.; Li, H.W. 2002. Landscapes to riverscapes: bridging the gap between research and conservation of stream fishes. BioScience 52: 483-498.

Fitzpatrick, F.A.; Diebel, M.W.; Harris, M.A.; [and others]. 2005. Effects of urbanization on the geomorphology, habitat, hydrology and fish index of biotic integrity in streams in the Chicago area, Illinois and Wisconsin. In: Brown, L.R.; Gray, R.H.; Hughes, R.M.; Meador, M.R. eds. Effects of urbanization on stream ecosystems. American Fisheries Society Symposium 47. Bethesda, MD: American Fisheries Society: 87-115.

Flather, C. H.; Hoekstra, T.W. 1989. An analysis of the wildlife and fish situation in the United States: 1989-2040. Gen. Tech. Rep. RM-178. Fort Collins, CO: U.S. Department of Agriculture, Forest Service, Rocky Mountain Forest and Range Experiment Station. 146 p.

Flebbe, P.A.; Dolloff, C.A. 1995. Trout use of woody debris and habitat in Appalachian wil-derness streams of North Carolina. North American Journal of Fisheries Management 15: 579-590.

Garie, H.L.; McIntosh, A. 1986. Distribution of benthic macroinvertebrates in a stream exposed to urban runoff. Water Resources Bulletin 22: 447-455.

Good, T.P.; Waples, R.S.; Adams P., (eds.). 2005. Updated status of federally listed ESUs of west coast salmon and steelhead. U.S. Department of Commerce, NOAA Tech. Memo., NMFS-NWFSC-66. 598 p.

Gutzwiller, K.J.; Flather, C.H. 2011. Wetland features and landscape context predict the risk of wetland habitat loss. Ecological Applications 21: 968-982.

Hansen, M.J.; Schorfhaar, R.G.; Peck, J.W.; [and others]. 1995. Abundance indices for determining the status of lake trout restoration in Michigan waters of Lake Superior. North American Journal of Fisheries Management 15: 830-837.

Hari, R. E.; Livingstone, D. M.; Siber, R.; [and others]. 2006. Consequences of climatic change for water temperature and brown trout populations in alpine rivers and streams. Global Change Biology 12: 10-26.

Hasler, C.T.; Christie, G.C.; Imhof, J.; [and others]. 2011. A network approach to addressing strategic fisheries, aquaculture, and aquatic sciences issues at a national scale: An Introduction to a series of case studies from Canada. Fisheries 36: 450-453.

Havel, J.E.; Lee, C.E.; Vander Zanden, M.J. 2005. Do reservoirs facilitate invasions into landscapes? BioScience 55: 518-525.

Heino, J.; Virkkala, R.; Toivonen, H. 2009. Climate change and freshwater biodiversity: detected patterns, future trends and adaptations in northern regions. Biological Reviews 84: 39-54.

Helms, J.A., ed. 1998. The dictionary of forestry. Washington, DC: Society of American Foresters. 210 p.

Hollis, G.E. 1975. The effects of urbanization on floods of different reoccurrence interval. Water Resources Research 11: 431-435.

International Joint Commission. 2011. 15th biennial report on Great Lakes water quality. Washington, DC: International Joint Commission, United States Section; Ottawa, Ontario: International Joint Commission, Canadian Section. 59 p.

Irons, K.S.; Sass, G.G.; McClelland, M.A.; Stafford, J.D. 2007. Reduced condition factor of two native fish species coincident with invasion of non-native Asian carps in the Illinois River, U.S.A. Is this evidence of competition and reduced fitness? Journal of Fish Biology 71 (suppl D): 258-273.

Isaak , D.J.; Luce, C.H.; Rieman, B.E.; [and others]. 2010. Effects of climate change and wildfire on stream temperatures and salmonid thermal habitat in a mountain river network. Ecological Applications 20: 1350–1371.

Jelks, H.L.; Walsh, S.J.; Burkhead, N.M.; [and others]. 2008. Conservation status of imperiled North American freshwater and diadromous fishes. Fisheries 33: 372-407.

Julius, S.H.; West, J.M., (eds.). 2008. Preliminary Review of adaptation options for climate-sensitive ecosystems and resources. U.S. Climate Change Science Program and the Subcommittee on Global Change Research Final Report. Synthesis and Assessment Product 4.4 June 2008. Washington, DC: U.S. Environmental Protection Agency. 873 p.

Karl, T.R.; Melillo, J.M.; Peterson, T.C., (eds). 2009. Global climate change impacts in the United States. Cambridge University Press. 196 p.

Kennan, J.G.; Chang, M.; Tracy, B.H. 2005. Effects of landscape change on fish assemblage structure in a rapidly growing metropolitan area in North Carolina. In: Brown, L.R.; Gray, R.H.; Hughes, R.M.; Meador, M.R., eds. Effects of urbanization on stream ecosystems. American Fisheries Society Symposium 47. Bethesda, MD: American Fisheries Society: 39-52

Loftus, A.J., (ed.). 2006. Proceedings of the National Fisheries Data Summit. Bethesda, MD: American Fisheries Society Computer User Section. 56 p.

Loftus, A.J.; Beard, T.D. 2009. The Multistate Aquatic Resources Information System (MARIS): Sharing data across agency boundaries. In: Bonar, S.A.; Hubert, W.A.; Willis, D.W., eds. Standard methods for sampling North American freshwater fishes. Bethesda, MD: American Fisheries Society: 187.

Loftus, A.J.; Flather C.H. 2000. Fish and other aquatic resource trends in the United States: A technical document supporting the 2000 USDA Forest Service RPA Assessment. Gen. Tech. Rep. RMRS-GTR-53. Fort Collins, CO. U.S. Department of Agriculture, Forest Service, Rocky Mountain Research Station. 50 p.

Mac, M.J.; Opler, P.A.; Puckett Haecker, C.E.; Doran, P.D. 1998. Status and trends of the nation's biological resources. 2 vols. Reston, VA: U.S. Department of the Interior, U.S. Geological Survey.

McInerny, M.C.; Cross, T.K. 2000. Effects of sampling time, intraspecific density, and environmental variables on electrofishing catch per effort of largemouth bass in Minnesota lakes. North American Journal of Fisheries Management 20: 328-336.

Miller, D.; Luce, C.; Benda, L. 2003. Time, space, and episodicity of physical disturbance in streams. Forest Ecology and Management 178: 89-104.

Nate, N.A.; Bozek, M.A.; Hansen, M.J.; [and others]. 2003. Predicting the occurrence and success of walleye populations from physical and biological features of northern Wisconsin lakes. North American Journal of Fisheries Management 23: 1207-1214.

National Fish Habitat Board. 2010. Through a fish's eye: The status of fish habitats in the United States 2010. Washington DC: Association of Fish and Wildlife Agencies. 68 p.

National Marine Fisheries Service (NMFS). 1971–1975. Fishery statistics of the United States. Washington, DC: U.S. Department of Commerce, National Oceanic and Atmospheric Administration, National Marine Fisheries Service.

National Marine Fisheries Service (NMFS). 1976a. Fisheries of the United States, 1975. Washington, DC: U.S. Department of Commerce, National Oceanic and Atmospheric Administration, National Marine Fisheries Service. 100 p.

National Marine Fisheries Service (NMFS). 1976b. Fishery statistics of the United States, 1973. Washington, DC: U.S. Department of Commerce, National Oceanic and Atmospheric Administration, National Marine Fisheries Service. 458 p.

National Marine Fisheries Service (NMFS). 1977. Fishery statistics of the United States, 1974. Washington, DC: U.S. Department of Commerce, National Oceanic and Atmospheric Administration, National Marine Fisheries Service. 424 p.

National Marine Fisheries Service (NMFS). 1978. Fishery statistics of the United States, 1975. Washington, DC: U.S. Department of Commerce, National Oceanic and Atmospheric Administration, National Marine Fisheries Service. 418 p.

National Marine Fisheries Service (NMFS). 1979. Fisheries of the United States, 1978. Washington, DC: U.S. Department of Commerce, National Oceanic and Atmospheric Administration, National Marine Fisheries Service. 120 p.

National Marine Fisheries Service (NMFS). 1980a. Fisheries of the United States, 1979. Washington, DC: U.S. Department of Commerce, National Oceanic and Atmospheric Administration, National Marine Fisheries Service. 131 p.

National Marine Fisheries Service (NMFS). 1980b. Fishery statistics of the United States, 1976. Washington, DC: U.S. Department of Commerce, National Oceanic and Atmospheric Administration, National Marine Fisheries Service. 419 p.

National Marine Fisheries Service (NMFS). 1981–1983. Fisheries of the United States. Washington, DC: U.S. Department of Commerce, National Oceanic and Atmospheric Administration, National Marine Fisheries Service.

National Marine Fisheries Service (NMFS). 1984a. Fisheries of the United States, 1983. Washington, DC: U.S. Department of Commerce, National Oceanic and Atmospheric Administration, National Marine Fisheries Service. 121 p.

National Marine Fisheries Service (NMFS). 1984b. Fishery statistics of the United States, 1977. Washington, DC: U.S. Department of Commerce, National Oceanic and Atmospheric Administration, National Marine Fisheries Service. 407 p.

National Marine Fisheries Service (NMFS). 1985–1996. Fisheries of the United States. Washington, DC: U.S. Department of Commerce, National Oceanic and Atmospheric Administration, National Marine Fisheries Service.

National Marine Fisheries Service (NMFS). 2000. Viable Salmonid populations and the recovery of evolutionarily significant units. NOAA Tech. Memo. NMFS-NWFSC-42. Washington, DC: U.S. Department of Commerce, National Oceanic and Atmospheric Administration, National Marine Fisheries Service. 174p.

National Marine Fisheries Service (NMFS). 2007. Fisheries economics of the United States 2006. Silver Spring, MD: U.S. Department of Commerce, National Oceanic and Atmospheric Administration, National Marine Fisheries Service, Office of Science and Technology. 166p.

National Marine Fisheries Service (NMFS). 2008. 2007 Status of U.S. Fisheries. Annual Report to Congress on the Status of U.S. Fisheries-2008. Silver Spring, MD: U.S. Department of Commerce, National Oceanic and Atmospheric Administration, National Marine Fisheries Service, Office of Science and Technology. 27 p.

National Marine Fisheries Service (NMFS). 2009a. Fisheries of the United States 2008. Silver Spring, MD: U.S. Department of Commerce, National Oceanic and Atmospheric Administration, National Marine Fisheries Service, Office of Science and Technology. 118 p.

National Marine Fisheries Service (NMFS). 2009b. 2008 Status of U.S. Fisheries. Annual Report to Congress on the Status of U.S. Fisheries-2008. Silver Spring, MD: U.S. Department of Commerce, National Oceanic and Atmospheric Administration, National Marine Fisheries Service, Office of Science and Technology. 23 p.

National Marine Fisheries Service (NMFS). 2010a. 2010 Report to Congress: Pacific Coastal Salmon Recovery Fund FY2000-FY2009. Silver Spring, MD: U.S. Department of Commerce, National Oceanic and Atmospheric Administration, National Marine Fisheries Service, Office of Science and Technology. 16 p.

National Marine Fisheries Service (NMFS). 2010b. 2009 Status of U.S. Fisheries Annual Report to Congress on the Status of U.S. Fisheries-2009. Silver Spring, MD: U.S. Department of Commerce, National Oceanic and Atmospheric Administration, National Marine Fisheries Service, Office of Science and Technology. 28 p.

National Marine Fisheries Service (NMFS). 2010c. Fisheries Economics of the United States, 2009. NOAA Tech. Memo. NMFS-F/SPO-118. Silver Spring, MD: U.S. Department of Commerce, National Oceanic and Atmospheric Administration, National Marine Fisheries Service, Office of Science and Technology. 172p.

National Marine Fisheries Service (NMFS). 2010d. Fisheries of the United States. 2009. Silver Spring, MD: U.S. Department of Commerce, National Oceanic and Atmospheric Administration, National Marine Fisheries Service, Office of Science and Technology. 118 p.

NatureServe. 2010. NatureServe Central Databases—10/13/10. NatureServe, Arlington, VA. Metadata on file with Curtis H. Flather, Rocky Mountain Research Station, Fort Collins, CO.

Nehlsen, W.; Williams, J.E.; Lichatowich, J.A. 1991. Pacific salmon at the crossroads: Stocks at risk from California, Oregon, Idaho, and Washington. Fisheries 16(2) 4-21.

Nelson, K.C.; Palmer, M.A.; Pizzuto, J.E.; [and others]. 2009. Forecasting the combined effects of urbanization and climate change on stream ecosystems: From impacts to management options. Journal of Applied Ecology 46: 154-163.

Piccolo, J.J; Adkison, M.D.; Rue, F. 2009. Linking Alaskan salmon fisheries management with ecosystem-based escapement goals: A review and prospectus. Fisheries 34: 124-134.

Radeloff, V.C.; Stewart, S.I.; Hawbaker, T.J.; [and others]. 2010. Housing growth in and near United States protected areas limits their conservation value. Proceedings of the National Academy of Sciences of the United States of America 107: 940-945.

Rahel, F.J. 2002. Homogenization of freshwater faunas. Annual Review of Ecology and Systematics 33: 291-315.

Rasmussen, J.L.; Regier, H.A.; Sparks, R.E.; Taylor, W.W. 2011. Dividing the waters: The case for hydrologic separation of the North American Great Lakes and Mississippi River basins. Journal of Great Lakes Research 37: 588-592.

Rieman, B.E.; Isaak, D.J. 2010. Climate change, aquatic ecosystems, and fishes in the Rocky Mountain West: Implications and alternatives for management. Gen. Tech. Rep. RMRS-GTR-250. Fort Collins, CO: U.S. Department of Agriculture, Forest Service, Rocky Mountain Research Station. 46 p.

Riitters, K.H.; Wickham, J.D. 2003. How far to the nearest road? Frontiers in Ecology and the Environment 1: 125-129.

Saunders, S.; Montgomery, C.; Easley, T.; Spencer, T. 2008. Hotter and drier: The West's changed climate. [Online]. The Rocky Mountain Climate Organization. Available: http://www.rockymountainclimate.org/ [March, 2008].

Sax, D.F.; Smith, K.F.; Thompson, A.R. 2009. Managed relocation: A nuanced evaluation is needed. Trends in Ecology and Evolution 24: 472-473.

Schindler, D.E.; Augerot, X.; Fleishman, E.; [and others]. 2008. Climate change, ecosystem impacts, and management for Pacific salmon. Fisheries 33: 502-506.

Solomon, S.; Qin, D.; Manning, M.; [and others], (eds). 2007. Climate change 2007: The physical science basis. Contribution of Working Group I to the Fourth Assessment Report of the Intergovernmental Panel on Climate Change. New York: Cambridge University Press. 996 pp.

Southwick Associates. 2008. Sportfishing in America: An economic engine and conservation powerhouse. Produced for the American Sportfishing Association with funding from the Multistate Conservation Grant Program, Alexandria, VA. 12 p.

Spangler, G.R.; Collins, J.J. 1992. Lake Huron fish community structure based on gill-net catches corrected for selectivity and encounter probabilities. North American Journal of Fisheries Management 12: 585–597.

Steedman, R.J. 1988. Modification and assessment of an index of biotic integrity to quantify stream quality in southern Ontario. Canadian Journal of Fisheries and Aquatic Sciences 45: 492-501.

Stynes, D.J.; White, E.M. 2006. Spending profiles of National Forest visitors, NVUM four year Report. USDA Forest Service and Michigan State University. 26 p.

Thayer, S.; Loftus, A.J. 2012. Great Lakes recreational fisheries and their role in resource management and policy. In: Taylor, W.W.; Lynch, A.J.; Leonard, N.J. (eds). Great Lakes fisheries policy and management: A binational perspective. East Lansing, MI: Michigan State University press: 399-439.

U.S. Department of Agriculture, Forest Service. 1977. The nation's renewable resources—an assessment, 1975. Forest Resource Report No. 21. Washington, DC: U.S. Government Printing Office. 243 p.

U.S. Department of the Interior. 1967–1969. Fishery statistics of the United States. Washington, DC: U.S. Department of the Interior, Bureau of Commercial Fisheries.

U.S. Department of the Interior, Fish and Wildlife Service; U.S. Department of Commerce, U.S. Census Bureau (USDI and USDC). 2007. 2006 National survey of fishing, hunting, and wildlife-associated recreation. 164 p.

U.S. Environmental Protection Agency (USEPA). 2006. Wadeable streams assessment: a collaborative survey of the nation's streams. EPA 841-B-06-002. Washington, DC: U.S. Environmental Protection Agency, Office of Research and Development, Office of Water. 98 p.

U.S. Environmental Protection Agency (USEPA). 2008. National coastal condition report III. EPA/842-R-08-002. Washington, DC: U.S. Environmental Protection Agency, Office of Research and Development, Office of Water. 329 p.

U.S. Environmental Protection Agency (USEPA). 2009. 2008 Biennial national listing of fish advisories. EPA-823-F-09-007. Washington, DC: U.S. Environmental Protection Agency, Office of Research and Development, Office of Water. 7 p.

U.S. Environmental Protection Agency (USEPA). 2009. National lakes assessment: A collaborative survey of the nation's lakes. EPA 841-R-09-001. Washington, DC: U.S. Environmental Protection Agency, Office of Research and Development, Office of Water. 102 p.

U.S. Environmental Protection Agency; Environment Canada. 2009. State of the Great Lakes Highlights 2009. Washington, DC: U.S. Environmental Protection Agency; Gatineau, Quebec, Canada: Environment Canada. 16 p. Online: http://binational.net/solec/sogl2009/sogl_2009_h_en.pdf. October 20, 2011.

U.S. Geological Survey. 2005. Mycobacteriosis in striped bass. Fact Sheet FHB 2002-01. Kearneysville, WV: U.S. Department of the Interior, U.S. Geological Survey, Fish Health Branch. 2 p.

Wang, L.; Infante, D.; Esselman, P.; [and others]. 2011. A hierarchical spatial framework and database for the national river fish habitat condition assessment. Fisheries 36: 436-449.

Ward, C.; Eshenroder, R.L.; Bence, J.R. 2000. Relative abundance of lake trout and burbot in the main basin of Lake Michigan in the early 1930s. Transactions of the American Fisheries Society 129: 282–295.

Weber, W.G.; Reed, L.A. 1976. Sediment runoff during highway construction. Civil Engineering 46: 76-79.

Wenger, S.J.; Isaak, D.J.; Luce, C.H.; [and others]. 2011. Flow regime, temperature, and biotic interactions drive differential declines of trout species under climate change. Proceedings of the National Academy of Sciences 108: 14175-14180.

Wheeler, A.P.; Angermeier, P.L.; Rosenberger A.E. 2005. Impacts of new highways and subsequent landscape urbanization on stream habitat and biota. Reviews in Fisheries Science 13: 141-164.

Williams, J.E.; Johnson, J.E.; Hendrickson, D.A.; [and others]. 1989. Fishes of North America endangered, threatened, or of special concern: 1989. Fisheries 14(6): 2-20.

Appendix A. Glossary of terms used in the text_____

anadromous—fish that migrate up river from the sea to spawn

at-risk species—a species whose biological and ecological circumstances place it at a very high (critically imperiled), high (imperiled), or moderate (vulnerable) risk of extinction based on the criteria specified by the conservation ranks developed by NatureServe (NatureServe 2010)

best management practices—a practice or usually a combination of practices that are determined by a state or designated planning agency to be the most effective and practicable means (including technological, economic, and institutional considerations) of controlling point and nonpoint source pollution at levels compatible with environmental goals (Helms 1998)

biotic—living component of the community

biotic condition—see "index of biotic condition"

biological integrity—state of being capable of supporting and maintaining a balanced community of organisms having a species composition, diversity, and functional organization comparable to that of the natural habitat of the region (EPA 2006)

catchability—the susceptibility of an organism to be captured by a specific gear type

catch-per-unit-effort—the number of organisms captured per unit of time, space, or measure of gear

cyanobacteria—a phylum of bacteria that obtain their energy through photosynthesis – also known as blue-green algae

designated use—water quality standards that define the goals for a water body by designating its highest attainable uses

diadromous—an organism that migrates between fresh and salt water

distinct population segment—vertebrate population or group of populations that is discrete from other populations of the species and significant in relation to the entire species

ecoregion—a geographic area a defined by its environmental conditions (for example, climate, landforms, soil characteristics)

ecosystem—a complex set of relationships among the living resources and physical environment of an area

ecosystem services/ecological services—the conditions and processes through which natural ecosystems, and the species which make them up, sustain and fulfill human life (Daily 1997)

endangered—an animal or plant species in danger of extinction throughout all or a significant portion of its range

evolutionarily significant unit—a population or group of populations that is substantially reproductively isolated from other conspecific populations and that represents an important component of the evolutionary legacy of the species

exclusive economic zone—the area of the ocean over which a nation has special rights over the exploration and use of marine resources, generally stretching a distance of 200 nautical miles from its coast

expenditures—money spent on fishing-related recreational trips and equipment in the United States and includes money spent by participants for themselves, or the value of gifts received by a participant

extinct—a species that no longer exists

federal trust species—species designated as threatened or endangered under the Endangered Species Act as well as migratory birds (for example, waterfowl, wading birds, shore-birds, neotropical migratory songbirds)

habitat—the environment of an animal, plant, or other organism

imperiled—at risk of becoming threatened, endangered, or extinct

index of biotic condition—the sum of a number of individual measures of biological condi-tion, such as the number of taxa in a sample, the number of taxa with different habits and feeding strategies, etc. (EPA 2006)

Interstate Fisheries Commission—any of three marine fisheries commissions established through a compact of states and approved by the Congress for the purposes of coordi-nating management of interjurisdictional marine resources

invertebrate—an animal without a backbone or spinal column

landscape—physical features of an area of land

lentic—standing water, such as a lake or pond

livebearers—a fish that bear live young rather than depositing eggs

lotic—moving water, such as a stream or river

macroinvertebrate—invertebrate animal large enough to be seen without the aid of a dissecting scope

maximum sustainable yield—the theoretical largest harvest that can be taken from a species' stock over an indefinite period without threatening the ability of the stock to replenish itself

microcystin—nonribosomal peptides produced by cyanobacteria that can be very toxic for plants and animals (including humans)

mycobacteriosis—a generic term that describes a tuberculosis-like disease caused by a group of bacteria known as mycobacteria that predominantly affect the visceral organs of striped bass and can also cause unsightly skin ulcers

observed/expected ratio—the number of species observed divided by the number of species in a reference condition

overfished—fish population levels that are below that which can replenish itself

overfishing—the rate of fishery removals, or fishing mortality, is too high to sustain the current fishing levels and allow the stock to replenish itself—a stock may be subject to "overfishing" but not yet be "overfished"

participant—for the National Survey of Fishing, Hunting, and Wildlife-Associated Recreation, participant is an individual who reported engaging in recreational fishing during the survey year

riparian—a zone or area that is the interface between land and a watercourse (river, lake, or stream) that is often characterized by hydrophilic plants

subspecies—an organism identified below the species level on the phylogenetic scale

sustainable—a method of harvesting or using a resource so that the resource is not depleted or permanently damaged and is capable of replenishing itself

taxon (pl. taxa)—a taxonomically defined group of organisms

threatened—an animal or plant species likely to become endangered within the foreseeable future throughout all or a significant portion of its range

urbanization—a process in which an increasing proportion of a population lives in cities and the suburbs of cities

Appendix B: Scientific names of species mentioned in the text _____

American eel—*Anguilla rostrata*

American lobster—*Homarus americanus*

American shad—*Alosa sapidissima*

Asian Carp—*Hypophthalmichthys nobilis* or *Hypophthalmichthys molitrix*

Atantic Menhaden —*Brevoortia tyrannus*

Atlantic Salmon—*Salmo salar*

Atlantic Sturgeon—*Acipenser oxyrinchus*

Black Bass—*Micropterus salmoides* or *Micropterus dolomieu*

Brook Trout—*Salvelinus fontinalis*

Brown Trout—*Salmo trutta*

Bull Trout—*Salvelinus confluentus*

Bullhead —*Ameiurus* spp.

Catfish —*Ictalurus* spp.

Chinook/King Salmon—*Oncorhynchus tshawytscha*

Chum/Dog Salmon—*Oncorhynchus keta*

Clams—A marine or freshwater bivalve mollusk of the class Pelecypoda

Cod—*Gadus* spp.

Coho/Silver Salmon—*Oncorhynchus kisutch*

Crappie—*Pomoxis* spp.

Crustaceans—Aquatic arthropods of the class Crustacea

Cutthroat Trout—*Oncorhynchus clarkii*

Darters—A small North American fish of the genera *Etheostoma*, *Ammocrypta*, or *Percina*

Eurasian watermilfoil—*Myriophyllum spicatum*

Finfish—An aquatic vertebrate of the class Osteichthyes with two sets of paired fins and several unpaired fins

Flatfish—An aquatic vertebrate of the order Pleuronectiformes

Halibut (Pacific)—*Hippoglossus stenolepis*

Herring—*Clupea* spp.

Horseshoe Crab—*Limulus polyphemus*

Lake Trout—*Salvelinus namaycush*

Largemouth Bass—*Micropterus salmoides*

Pacific Salmon—fish of the genus *Oncorhynchus*

Panfish—A generic name referring to a small fish suitable for frying, in this case generally
Perca spp., *Pomoxis* spp., or *Lepomis* spp.

Pink/Humpback Salmon—*Oncorhynchus gorbushca*

Pollock—*Theragra* spp.

Pupfish—*Cyprinodon* spp.

Quagga Mussel—*Dreissena rostriformis bugensis*

Rainbow Trout—*Oncorhynchus mykiss*

Round Goby—*Neogobius melanostomus*

Salmon (Pacific, western, northwestern)—*Oncorhynchus* spp.

Sardines—Fish of the family Clupiedae

Scallops—*Placopecten magellanicus*

Sea Lamprey—*Petromyzon marinus*

Sea-run Cutthroat Trout—*Oncorhynchus clarkii clarkii*

Shellfish—An aquatic shelled mollusk or crustacean

Smallmouth Bass—*Micropterus dolomieu*

Snails—An aquatic or terrestrial mollusks of the class Gastropoda

Snapping Turtle—*Chelydra* spp.

Sockeye Salmon—*Oncorhynchus nerka*

Spiny Waterflea—*Bythotrephes longimanus*

Steelhead Trout—*Oncorhynchus mykiss*

Striped Bass—*Marone saxatilis*

Summer Flounder—*Paralichthys dentatus*

Trout—Any of several chiefly freshwater game fish of the genera *Oncorhynchus*, *Salvelinus*,
or *Salmo*

Walleye—*Sander vitreus*

Walleye Pollock—*Theragra chalcogramma*

Weakfish—*Cynoscion regalis*

White Bass—*Morone chrysops*

Yellow Perch—*Perca flavescens*

Zebra Mussel—*Dreissena polymorpha*

Appendix C: Source Data for Figure 3_____

Status of the biological condition of wadeable streams, by ecoregion in the United States based on Macroinvertebrate Index of Biotic Condition (MIBC) (USEPA 2006).

Region	Stream miles (x 1000)	Condition (% of stream miles)		
		Good	Fair	Poor
Nationwide	671.1	28	25	42
Northern Appalachians	97.9	13	15	45
Southern Appalachians	178.4	21	24	55
Coastal Plains	72.1	36	23	39
Upper Midwest	36.5	28	31	39
Temperate Plains	100.9	26	36	37
Southern Plains	19.3	22	20	54
Northern Plains	13.4	30	13	50
Western Mountains	126.4	46	28	25
Xeric West/Southwest	26.0	42	15	39

Appendix D: Source Data for Figure 4_____

Macroinvertebrate taxa loss determined by the ratio of observed number of species to the number of species expected at least-disturbed reference sites (O/E ratio) in wadeable streams by ecoregions in the United States (USEPA 2006).

Region	Stream miles (x 1000)	Percent of stream miles with:			
		>50% taxa loss	20% – 50% taxa loss	10% – <20% taxa loss	<10% taxa loss
Nationwide	671.1	13	26	12	41
Northern Appalachian	97.9	19	17	14	23
Southern Appalachian	178.4	16	36	13	30
Coastal Plains	72.1	15	38	12	32
Upper Midwest	36.5	5	31	18	45
Temperate Plains	100.9	10	17	12	58
Southern Plains	19.3	15	15	20	42
Northern Plains	13.4	12	16	6	60
Western Mountains	126.4	5	18	10	63
Xeric West/Southwest	26.0	15	35	10	34

www.ingramcontent.com/pod-product-compliance
Lightning Source LLC
Chambersburg PA
CBHW081230280526
45787CB00006B/2599